CARTESIAN LOGIC

Cartesian Logic

AN ESSAY ON DESCARTES'S CONCEPTION OF INFERENCE

Stephen Gaukroger

CLARENDON PRESS · OXFORD

1989

Oxford University Press, Walton Street, Oxford OX2 6DP

Oxford New York Toronto
Delhi Bombay Calcutta Madras Karachi
Petaling Jaya Singapore Hong Kong Tokyo
Nairobi Dar es Salaam Cape Town
Melbourne Auckland

and associated companies in
Berlin Ibadan

Oxford is a trade mark of Oxford University Press

Published in the United States
by Oxford University Press, New York

British Library Cataloguing in Publication Data
Gaukroger, Stephen
Cartesian logic : an essay on Descartes's
conception of inference.
1. French philosophy. Descartes, René
– 1650
I. Title
194
ISBN 0–19–824825–3

Library of Congress Cataloging in Publication Data
Gaukroger, Stephen
Cartesian logic.
Bibliography.   Includes index.
1. Descartes, René, 1596–1650—Contributions in logic
of inference. 2. Inference—History. I. Title.
B1878.I56G38 1989   160'.92'4   89–3070
ISBN 0–19–824825–3

Printed and bound in
Great Britain by Biddles Ltd,
Guildford and King's Lynn

To Gerd Buchdahl

Preface

This book grew out of two largely independent interests. The first was a concern with the justification of deduction, stimulated by Dummett's defence of an intuitionist logic and a constructivist semantics. This is an issue which is inseparable from developments in post-Fregean logic, as it presupposes both a fully algebraic conception of logic and an appreciation of the role of a sentential semantics in grasping the nature of deductive inference. But questions about the nature of inference have been posed since antiquity, and the more I thought about the problem the more I came to regret the fact that so little serious historical work had been done on how conceptions of inference had changed and on how current concerns about the nature of inference had been shaped. My second set of concerns derived from an interest in the development of mechanism in the seventeenth century. I had struck a number of problems about how inferential processes were to be conceived in the context of the dualism which, I believe, grew largely out of mechanism in this period. There was a very strong tendency to think of them in terms of the functioning of corporeal organs, which was contrary to what I had expected. Moreover, it soon became clear that concern with questions of method in the seventeenth century was very closely tied to problems about the nature of inference. At this point my two interests merged, and this book is the result.

Many people have helped this project along, but I would particularly like to thank John Bacon, Desmond Clarke, Nick Jardine, Charles Larmore, Lloyd Reinhardt, and John Yolton for comments and constructive criticism.

Parts of Chapter 2 originally appeared in an earlier version as 'Descartes' Conception of Inference', in R. Woolhouse (ed.), *Metaphysics and the Philosophy of Science in the Seventeenth and*

Eighteenth Centuries (Dordrecht, 1988). I am grateful to the publishers and copyright holders, Kluwer Academic Publishers, for permission to use this material.

S.G.

Sydney
1988

Contents

Abbreviations

AT   *Œuvres de Descartes*, ed. Charles Adam and Paul Tannery (11 vols., Paris, 1974–86).

C   *Opuscules et fragments inédits de Leibniz*, ed. Louis Couturat (Paris, 1903).

EW   *The English Works of Thomas Hobbes*, ed. Sir William Molesworth (11 vols., London, 1839–45).

GM   *Die mathematische Schriften von G. W. Leibniz*, ed. C. I. Gerhardt (7 vols., Berlin and Halle, 1849–63).

GP   *Die philosophische Schriften von G. W. Leibniz*, ed. C. I. Gerhardt (7 vols., Berlin, 1875–90).

In the case of abbreviations of classical titles, I have followed those used in Liddell and Scott's *Greek–English Lexicon* (9th edition, Oxford, 1978) and Lewis and Short's *Latin Dictionary* (Oxford, 1980).

It is idle to expect any great advances in science from the superinducing and engrafting of new things upon old. We must begin anew from the very foundations, unless we would revolve further in a circle with mean and contemptible progress. The honour of the ancient authors, and indeed of all, remains untouched; since the comparison I challenge is not of wits or faculties, but of ways and methods, and the part I take upon myself is not that of a judge, but of a guide. This must be plainly avowed: no judgement can be rightly formed either of my method or of the discoveries to which it leads, by means of anticipations (that is to say, of the reasoning which is now in use); since I cannot be called on to abide by the sentence of a tribunal which is itself on trial. (Francis Bacon, *Novum organum*, xxxi–xxxii.)

Introduction

THE period between the final decline of medieval logic around the beginning of the sixteenth century and the publication of Boole's *Mathematical Analysis of Logic* in 1847 is generally seen as an interregnum in the history of logic. Three areas in the development of logic in this period can be distinguished: the development of semantics, the development of increasingly general and abstract systems of deductive inference, and the development of conceptions of the nature of inference. In regard to semantics, this is generally seen as the most fruitful area of the three in this period, although semantics develops in the main quite independently of a more general interest in logical questions, and after Terminist logic it is not really until Frege that semantics is fully reintegrated into logic.[1] As regards the second set of concerns, the period is indeed an interregnum, especially when compared with the great era of medieval logic from the mid-twelfth to the mid-fifteenth centuries, and developments in logic from Frege onwards. This is in spite of the efforts of Leibniz, Euler, Gergonne, Hamilton, and others, efforts which remained isolated from the mainstream of logic in this period.[2] The third set of concerns is more difficult to assess. What is involved is philosophical questions about what inference consists in, whether it can be justified or explained or clarified in more fundamental terms, in what sense inference can be informative, and so on. These issues have been neglected in

[1] See N. Kretzman, 'Semantics, History of', in P. Edwards (ed.), *Encyclopedia of Philosophy* (8 vols., New York, 1967), vii. 358–406; specifically on the 17th cent. see E. J. Ashworth, *Language and Logic in the Post-Medieval Period* (Dordrecht, 1974).

[2] See W. and M. Kneale, *The Development of Logic* (Oxford, 1962), and N. I. Styazhkin, *History of Mathematical Logic from Leibniz to Peano* (Cambridge, Mass., 1969).

comparison with the first two sets of concerns, and there is a general assumption that nothing, or at least nothing of value, was achieved in this area in the 'interregnum' period. And the picture does indeed look bleak. Not only does there appear to be a general misunderstanding of the aims of Aristotelian syllogistic on the part both of its defenders and its detractors,[3] for example, but in place of the often plausible and attractive conceptions of antiquity we find the most apparently banal and bizarre views: that inference is simply a psychological process (late scholastics), that logical truths are such only because God has chosen to make them so (Descartes), or that formal reasoning is worthless (Locke).

My concern in this book is with the way in which Descartes deals with the philosophical questions of inference. His treatment of this whole area was extremely influential, an influence exerted not just through his own writings such as the *Discourse on Method*, but also through the versions of the Cartesian conception of logic offered in Arnauld and Nicole's *Port-Royal Logic*, and in Locke's *Essay*. That Descartes's conception of inference has largely been ignored in histories of logic is, however, not as surprising as it may at first seem. The problem (as far as historians of logic are concerned) is, I believe, that the context in which questions of inference are raised is not an explicitly logical one, but usually one dominated by a concern with issues of scientific discovery, although they may also be raised in the context of concerns in theology, theories of cognition, pedagogy, and so on. This poses immense interpretative problems since the context of argumentation is often obscure, and the accounts that Descartes is opposing often difficult to identify. Indeed, I shall argue that problems in this latter respect have been the cause of serious misunderstandings of Descartes's account of inference. But even where we can identify the relevant context of argumentation precisely, confusion can still arise from the way in which questions are posed, for the context often seems utterly inappropriate. It is very common to

---

[3] See W. S. Howell, *Eighteenth-Century British Logic and Rhetoric* (Princeton, 1971), ch. 2.

find questions about whether the conclusion of an argument tells us something different from the premises from which it is deduced, for example, being posed in the context of questions about what forms of enquiry or argument enable us to discover something (factually) new. This happens not just in the seventeenth century but in antiquity and right up until the nineteenth century. It is relatively easy to separate out two distinct questions here, but much more difficult to explain why they were persistently treated as the one question over such a long period.

Descartes's conception of inference is of interest not just because of its immense influence, but because it raises both logical and cognitive questions about what inference consists in, questions which are constitutive of modern problems about inference (e.g. about how inference can be informative) but which are largely absent in his immediate predecessors and which are posed in quite different ways in his remote predecessors. His account is actually a good deal more coherent than commentators have generally allowed, and he is instrumental in developing an understanding of inference which, for all its faults, is far superior to those which prevailed in the early seventeenth century. This fact has been overlooked because commentators have taken it that the alternative to Descartes's conception was that embodied in Aristotelian syllogistic.[4] But, in the first place, in so far as Descartes and his contemporaries are concerned with Aristotelian syllogistic, they are concerned with it as a procedure for scientific discovery, not as an account of valid inference patterns or as an account of what inference consists in. Secondly, at the level of philosophical questions about what inference is, Descartes's concern is with Ramist and late scholastic conceptions of inference, not with Aristotle's. A number of developments in medieval and Renaissance thought raised new problems about what and how we know which radically altered the way in which questions of inference came to be seen. This shift, from what I call a discursive to a

---

[4] A notable exception is W. Risse, 'Zur Vorgeschichte der cartesischen Methodenlehre', *Archiv für Geschichte der Philosophie*, 45 (1963), 269-91.

facultative conception of inference,[5] effectively precluded an Aristotelian solution to the problems.

Aristotelian syllogistic is the subject of the first chapter, where I look at the 'internal' criticisms of syllogistic up to Descartes's time. These criticisms are 'internal' in the sense that they are designed to show that syllogistic cannot do what it claims (or was thought to claim) to be able to do. They do not form the core of Descartes's objection to syllogistic, and in fact if one wants the details of the arguments one has to go to Sextus Empiricus rather than a seventeenth-century source, but they are taken up by Descartes and they give us a good idea of what Descartes and others in the seventeenth century expected of logic.

The core of his position is discussed in the second chapter, and this contains the crux of my own argument. There are two doctrines that have a bearing on Descartes's account of inference: his theory that inference must be grasped in an *intuitus*, and the doctrine that eternal truths are freely created by God. It is of paramount importance here that we appreciate that these are not part of the same doctrine, as has generally been supposed. The thrust of the first is that inference is simple and primitive, that it is neither further analysable nor, more importantly, reducible to psychological processes, pedagogic aids, or whatever. Here Descartes is specifically challenging identifiable contemporary views. The second doctrine, I argue, does not have any direct bearing on logical questions of inference, but it does have a bearing on the cognitive status of inference for, contrary to appearances, it enables Descartes to dissociate our reasoning processes from a divine model, and thereby provides a foundation for the primitiveness and intrinsic reliability of human reasoning processes. The

---

[5] I owe the term 'facultative' to J. G. Buickerood, 'The Natural History of the Understanding: Locke and the Rise of Facultative Logic in the Eighteenth Century', *History and Philosophy of Logic*, 6 (1985), 157–90, although Buickerood seems to take facultative logic as a post-Cartesian phenomenon whereas, as I understand it, it originates in the 16th cent. In my 'Descartes' Conception of Inference', in R. Woolhouse (ed.), *Metaphysics and the Philosophy of Science in the Seventeenth and Eighteenth Centuries* (Dordrecht, 1988), I used the word 'cognitive', but this now seems to me to be question-begging, as the discursive conception is no less cognitive, in a broad sense, than the facultative one.

general interpretation of Descartes's conception of inference that I offer is quite different from others that have been proposed, but I believe it enables us to make much greater sense of what has often seemed a baffling account.

In the third and fourth chapters, I examine apparent divergences between Descartes's overall conception of inference and his work in mathematics and natural philosophy respectively. Although Descartes derides formal reasoning, in his mathematical work he develops and deploys what is the paradigm of formal reasoning, algebra. He construes algebra as a problem-solving rather than a deductive process, however, and he does not make the connections between algebra, formal reasoning, and deduction that we might expect. His peculiar construal of algebra results from mathematical considerations showing that synthesis, which he associates with deduction, is unnecessary, and I explore the basis of these considerations. This provides a framework within which to compare his views on deduction with those of Leibniz, and the second part of the chapter is devoted to such a comparison. The problem in natural philosophy, which I look at in Chapter 4, is that Descartes appears to adopt a straightforwardly deductive approach (e.g. in the *Principles*) and explicitly to reject a problem-solving approach (e.g. in his criticisms of Galileo). This again would be at odds with his general conception of inference and with his specifically problem-solving and anti-deductive approach in mathematics, an area which supposedly provides the model for his other enterprises. But in fact his procedure in natural philosophy is reconcilable with his rejection of deduction, provided that we pay careful attention to the context of his statements. The difficulties lie rather in how we are to conceive of the epistemic value of deduction, for Descartes rejects the idea that the deduction of a conclusion from premises can ever result in an epistemic advance, but this is quite contrary to the evidence and goes beyond what he needs to defend his experimental and problem-solving approach.

Descartes and Traditional Syllogistic

THE syllogism, which had been constitutive of formal reasoning from Aristotle up until the late Middle Ages, was subjected to increasing criticism from the mid-sixteenth century onwards, and Descartes's criticisms of the syllogism in the *Discourse on Method* were taken by virtually all of his successors, from Arnauld and Locke up until the second half of the nineteenth century, to have demolished syllogistic reasoning. In assessing these criticisms, there are two sets of factors that need to be taken into account. First, the criticisms of syllogistic run together questions of deductive inference, scientific discovery, and a number of other issues. Second, the substance of the criticisms is rarely spelled out, presumably because it was assumed that their force was so obvious that little really needed to be said. Yet for us the criticisms are often obscure, and some reconstruction of the basis of the argument is necessary. In this chapter, I shall examine and assess two of the most important of these criticisms: the claim that the syllogism is a *petitio principii*, and the claim that it does not lead to new truths. Both these assert that, in a very broad sense, the syllogism is circular. Unlike some of the other criticisms of the syllogism that we find in Descartes—for example, the argument that syllogistic impedes the natural light of reason—these two are in many respects traditional criticisms, and by looking at the way in which they were traditionally conceived we can put more flesh on the seventeenth-century criticisms. Before doing this, however, it will be helpful to gain some idea of what exactly is, and is not, at issue.

THE SCOPE OF LOGIC

The study of logic in the seventeenth century covered not only deductively valid forms of inference but also, and much more importantly, what can be called the 'logic of discovery'. On this broad understanding of the term 'logic', Descartes is a formative figure in the development of logic. Blake, Buchdahl, Laudan, and others have shown the importance of Descartes's conception of hypotheses, 'inverse-deduction', and so on for the development of modern conceptions of method,[1] and Howell has argued that eighteenth- and nineteenth-century ideas on the logic of discovery can be traced directly back to Descartes, whose approach, as developed by Locke, Kames, Campbell, and Stewart, leads directly to Mill.[2] On the other hand, if we understand logic in the sense of the study of deductively valid forms of inference, then the generally accepted view is that Descartes's contribution is non-existent. There is a problem here. It is not that we cannot separate questions of deductive inference from questions of the logic of discovery, for we can: I have just done so. The problem is rather that if we are to learn anything from this exercise, it is important to understand why it is *we* who have to do the separating. The fortunes of deductive inference and the logic of discovery were linked not only by Descartes's predecessors—in antiquity, in the Middle Ages, and in the Renaissance—and by Descartes himself, but by his successors also. The fact is that criticisms of syllogistic reasoning, that is, deductive reasoning for all intents and purposes until the second half of the nineteenth century, are closely tied to the development of a logic of discovery. The latter develops very much as a response to, and trades upon criticisms of, the former. Locke, for example, actually does little more than develop

---

[1] R. Blake, C. Ducasse, and E. Madden, *Theories of Scientific Method* (Seattle, 1960), ch. 4; G. Buchdahl, 'Descartes' Anticipation of a "Logic of Scientific Discovery"', in A. C. Crombie (ed.), *Scientific Change* (London, 1963); G. Buchdahl, 'The Relevance of Descartes' Philosophy for Modern Philosophy of Science', *British Journal for the History of Science*, 1 (1963), 227–49; G. Buchdahl, *Metaphysics and the Philosophy of Science* (Oxford, 1969), ch. 3; L. Laudan, *Science and Hypothesis* (Dordrecht, 1981), ch. 3.
[2] W. S. Howell, *Eighteeenth-Century British Logic and Rhetoric* (Princeton, 1971), ch. 5.

criticisms learned from Descartes.[3] Lord Kames's *Introduction to the Art of Thinking* (1761) and George Campbell's *Philosophy of Rhetoric* (1776), although very influential texts in the development of inductive logic, exert this influence not by telling us much about induction but rather by telling us in great detail why syllogistic reasoning is of no use in advancing science.[4] Dugald Stewart's seminal work on inductive logic, the second volume of his *Elements of the Philosophy of the Human Mind* (1814), ties the strengths of inductive logic very closely to the weaknesses of syllogistic reasoning,[5] as does Mill's *System of Logic* (1843), whose criticisms of the syllogism are as well known as its inductive logic.

Our first concern will, therefore, be not to separate deductive logic from the 'logic of discovery', but rather to understand why and how they were so closely connected. Unless we understand this we will not be able to undertake the delicate task of separating them, and a delicate task it is, for we must at no stage lose sight of what logic is being asked to do, what inference is being asked to achieve.

The difficulty in separating questions of deductive inference from more broadly conceived notions of logic can be brought out by comparing the kind of approach we find in Descartes with that which we find in a number of humanist writers on rhetoric. One reason why one might want to broaden one's conception of logic beyond the study of formally valid inference patterns is that one might want to accommodate intuitively valid or reasonable or plausible or otherwise unobjectionable forms of inference which are not formally valid. Such arguments might be compelling in that they provide us with moral certainty, or good grounds for belief, or whatever. This is the motivation behind some of the humanist reforms of logic in the fifteenth and sixteenth centuries. Lorenzo Valla and others, for example, tried to provide a systematic account of forms of inference that resisted formalization, on the

[3] J. A. Passmore, 'Descartes, the British Empiricists and Formal Logic', *Philosophical Review*, 62 (1953), 545–53.
[4] See Howell, *Eighteenth-Century British Logic*, pp. 393 ff. on Kames and pp. 397 ff. on Campbell.
[5] Howell, *Eighteenth-Century British Logic*, pp. 414 ff.

grounds that argument is in fact almost always concerned with persuasion and probability rather than with certainty.[6] Valla takes his cue from Cicero and Quintilian, who are concerned as much as anything else with effective forms of legal argument, a context where absolute certainty is not usually forthcoming.

An account of this kind was developed in an interesting way in the sixteenth century, in reply to arguments inspired by Pyrrhonism.[7] Francesco Patrizzi, in his *Dialogues on History* (1560), for example, attempted to show that the historian can either be impartial, or informed, but not both. Patrizzi begins by rejecting secondary sources as virtual hearsay, and he divides primary sources into the partisan and the objective. Then, relying on a number of Machiavellian assumptions about the nature of rulers, he sets up a dichotomy between the partisan observer and the objective observer. Partisan observers (i.e., in this case, those sympathetic to the ruler), in virtue of being partisan, have access to the relevant information, because the ruler can rely on them, but because they are partisan they will not provide an objective rendering of this information. Objective observers (i.e., in this case, those who are prepared to be critical of the ruler if he merits it), on the other hand, being objective, will not have the ruler's confidence, and hence will not have access to the source of the relevant information. (If this seems far-fetched, imagine the situation of someone writing a history of the Provisional IRA.) Patrizzi's conclusion is that it is 'utterly and totally impossible for human actions to be known as they were actually done'. The sixteenth-century humanist responses to this challenge attempt to show that there are a number of ways in which we can establish credibility and plausibility, along the lines applied in law where, for example, we have doubts about a witness's credibility. In such cases, we take into account such factors as the probative value of

  [6] See L. Jardine, 'Humanism and the Teaching of Logic', in N. Kretzman, A. Kenny, and J. Pinborg (eds.), *The Cambridge History of Later Medieval Philosophy* (Cambridge, 1982), 797–807; L. Jardine, 'Lorenzo Valla: Academic Skepticism and the New Humanist Dialectic', in M. Burnyeat (ed.), *The Skeptical Tradition* (Berkeley, 1983), 253–86.
  [7] For details see J. H. Franklin, *Jean Bodin and the Sixteenth Century Revolution in the Methodology of Law and History* (New York, 1963), chs. 6–9.

reinforcing testimonies, and there are obvious parallels between, such cases in law and those cases where we are concerned with the reliability of historical records and testimonies. This is the response of such apologists for history as Melchior Cano, François Baudoin, and Jean Bodin. Their aim is to show that the sceptical challenges are not in fact threats to historical knowledge *per se*, but rather that they are problems about evidence and reliability which practitioners of the discipline will usually be best placed to deal with. They will have to be dealt with in ways which require a degree of probabilistic reasoning, but the problem here lies in our ability to assess degrees of probability in particular cases, and not in the fact that it is probabilistic rather than conclusive reasoning.

Nothing could be further from Descartes's approach. On his approach, the humanist would simply have been engaging in piecemeal responses, whereas what is required is a complete and wholly general answer to any conceivable form of scepticism. Descartes's model is not the legal one offered by the humanists, but an uncompromisingly geometrical one and although, as we shall see below (Chapters 3 and 4), it is not a deductive model, Descartes's aim is to achieve certainty. He is not concerned with plausibility or high probability: as he puts it in a letter to Mersenne of 5 October 1637, 'I treat almost as false whatever is merely probable' (AT i. 451). On the face of it, Descartes would appear to need a rather sharp distinction between the prototypical axiomatic and deductive system and those forms of argument which do not lead to certainty. And the problem then is that this seems to contradict his own running together of questions of deductive inference and the logic of discovery.

But in fact it does not, for the connection between the two lies at a wholly different level. This is why we must be careful to determine how the two are connected before we attempt to separate them. For Descartes, the connection lies in the area of questions about how inference can be informative: in what way does the conclusion of an argument tell us something different from the premises from which it is deduced? In Descartes, and indeed more generally in the seventeenth century, this question is posed in the context of questions about what forms of enquiry or argument enable us to discover something new. Our principal task in what follows is to understand how this comes about and what precisely it involves.

THE SYLLOGISM AS A *PETITIO PRINCIPII*

The criticism of the syllogism as a *petitio principii* is made in Rule 10 of the *Regulae* in a reasonably straightforward fashion:

We must note that the dialecticians are unable to devise by their rules any syllogism which has a true conclusion, unless they already have the whole syllogism, i.e. unless they have already ascertained in advance the very truth which is deduced in that syllogism. (AT x. 406.)

The criticism is repeated in Rule 13, where we are told that the dialecticians, 'in teaching their doctrine of the forms of the syllogism, assume that the terms or substance of their syllogisms are already known' (AT x. 430). After making these criticisms, Descartes moves in both cases directly to the observation that syllogisms cannot lead to new truths. But it is important that we keep two issues distinct: the question of the connection between premisses and conclusion in the syllogism, and the question of whether the syllogism advances knowledge. We shall be concerned for the moment with the first issue.

The criticism that the syllogism is question-begging is a traditional one, deriving from antiquity. Descartes does not spell out what precisely he sees as the problem, but he presumably has in mind these traditional criticisms. There were two texts which were well known from the sixteenth century onwards in which scepticism about logic is discussed: Cicero's *Academica* (Book II, §§ xiv–xxx) and Sextus Empiricus' *Outlines of Pyrrhonism* (*Outlines*, II, §§ 134–244; *Adversus mathematicos*, II, §§ 300–481).[8]

---

[8] For details of scepticism about logic see C. B. Schmitt, 'The Rediscovery of Ancient Scepticism in Modern Times', in M. Burnyeat (ed.), *The Skeptical Tradition* (Berkeley, 1983). Specifically on Cicero, see C. B. Schmitt, *Cicero scepticus* (The Hague, 1972). More generally see R. H. Popkin, *The History of Scepticism from Erasmus to Spinoza* (Berkeley, 1979).

Sextus' account is of special interest. The thrust of his argument is that any attempt to back up inference by proof must fail. To this end, he looks at a number of purported forms of proof, the most important of which are Stoic conditional arguments and the Aristotelian categorical syllogism. The argument in the former case turns on the Stoic distinction between concludent and non-concludent arguments. A concludent argument is one in which the conclusion holds in virtue of the truth of the premisses and the form of the inference from these premisses to the conclusion. Certain forms of inference—such as 'If the first, then the second; but the first; therefore the second'—are 'indemonstrables' or axioms, and sequences of statements conforming to these are concludent arguments, that is, formally valid arguments. With inconcludent arguments, on the other hand—arguments such as 'The first, so the second'—the premiss or premisses do not yield the conclusion, so the argument must be restructured, for instance by supplying an extra premiss. To take Sextus' example, A is a concludent argument whereas B is an inconcludent argument:

A:	If it is day, it is light	B: It is day	(1)
	It is day		(2)
	————————————	————————	
	It is light	It is light	(3)

The sceptical objection then runs as follows (*Outlines of Pyrrhonism*, II, § 159). Either (3) follows from (2) or it does not. If it does, then B is a concludent argument, for in B we simply infer (3) from (2). But if this is the case then (1) is clearly redundant. On the other hand, if (3) does not follow from (2) then (1) is false, since (1) clearly asserts that it does. In other words, proof is impossible: what A tells us over and above B is either redundant or false. Indeed, the problems are compounded for the Stoics because of their identification of validity with formal validity, and because they count arguments with redundant premisses as invalid, so by their own principles formally valid arguments will always either be invalid or have a false premiss.[9] As if this were not enough, Sextus then dishes out the same treatment to the categorical syllogism. The crux of the argument is that:

in the argument—'The just is fair, but the fair is good, therefore the just is good', either it is agreed and pre-evident that the 'fair is good', or it is disputed and is non-evident. But if it is non-evident, it will not be granted in the process of deduction, and consequently the syllogism will not be conclusive; while if it is pre-evident that whatsoever is fair is also without exception good, at the moment of stating that this particular thing is fair the fact that it is good is likewise implied, so that it is enough to put the argument in the form 'The just is fair, therefore the just is good', and the other premiss, in which it was stated that 'the fair is good' is redundant.[10]

These are genuinely challenging arguments, and it is difficult to meet them in a simple and direct way. One thing that is clear is that they cannot be met by providing examples of cases where the conclusion of a formally valid argument is not apparent from the premisses, for example, as with some geometrical demonstrations or 'Lewis Carroll' arguments.[11] Proofs are proofs irrespective of whether the conclusion is immediately evident from the premisses. Were we concerned with what might be termed the revelatory features of arguments then there might be grounds on which to prefer an inference of the form $<\{P\}, Q>$ to one of the form $<\{\ulcorner$ If P then $Q\urcorner, P\}, Q>$. But if we are concerned with the question of how premisses yield conclusions, then our concern will be with specifying all and only those inferences which, independently of the actual content of particular premisses and conclusions, are truth-preserving, and capturing those features which make them truth-preserving. And if this is our concern, then what

---

[9] Cf. J. Barnes, 'Proof Destroyed', in M. Schofield, M. Burnyeat, and J. Barnes (eds.), *Doubt and Dogmatism* (Oxford, 1980), 161–81.

[10] *Outlines of Pyrrhonism*, II, § 163; Loeb edn., trans. Bury (4 vols., Cambridge, Mass., 1933–9), i. 257.

[11] Sextus has, in any case, independent arguments against geometry; cf. *Adversus mathematicos*, III. Mueller provides an illuminating discussion in his 'Geometry and Scepticism', in J. Barnes, J. Brunschwig, M. Burnyeat, and M. Schofield (eds.), *Science and Speculation* (Cambridge, 1982), 69–95.

the sceptic dismisses as the question-begging quality of *modus ponens* we must consider its truth-preserving quality.

But how, more specifically, does one deal with the sceptic's challenge? One way in which one might be tempted to answer the sceptic here is to point out that the sceptical argument presupposes what it denies: it uses inferential principles which purport to prove a conclusion. For example, the conclusion that (1) is false if (3) does not follow from (2) requires a grasp of *modus ponens* (if one is to grasp the original inference) and *modus tollens* (if one is to grasp the *reductio*). But this is not an effective response. It fails to recognize the fact that the sceptic himself makes no knowledge claims. Scepticism works by taking the knowledge claims of others and showing that, by their own criteria, they cannot know what they claim to know. In the present case, the sceptical argument trades on the fact that the Stoics' own formal inferential principles can be used to show that these principles are invalid, by the Stoics' own criteria.

A more promising form of response is to argue that (1) is not an inference at all, whereas *B* is. The appearance that (1) is an inference arises from its 'if . . . then . . .' form. But not all propositions of this form are properly construed as inferences. Take the case of material implication, for example. We can write (1) as $\ulcorner P \supset Q \urcorner$ or as $\ulcorner \neg(P \,\&\, \neg Q) \urcorner$. The latter does not have the slightest appearance of an inference: it simply makes the statement that it cannot both be the case that P and not be the case that Q. To avoid confusion, we can reserve the sign '⊢' for inferences, so that *A* is of the form $\ulcorner \neg(P \,\&\, \neg Q), P \vdash Q \urcorner$, and *B* is of the form $\ulcorner P \vdash Q \urcorner$. Now Stoic conditionals are not in fact material conditionals (because Stoic logic is a relevance logic, we would expect something stronger than the material conditional), and in any case there are many problems about how to handle conditionals, exacerbated in those cases where they have false antecedents, so the simple formalization that I have offered does little more than suggest a general strategy. But this strategy is surely a sound one for, however one conceives of conditionals, to construe them all as being inferences is both unnecessary and looking for trouble: trouble that the sceptic is happy to provide.

General scepticism about proof is scepticism which equally affects both immediate inferences, such as $<P,P>$, and 'remote' ones, such as Euclid's proof of Pythagoras' Theorem in the *Elements*. Both are equally 'question-begging' in the strong sceptical sense. But there is another sense of the term 'question-begging' which is also compatible with Descartes's criticism of the syllogism as something which must have already ascertained the truth of what it deduces. Sextus gives an example of question-begging in this second sense, although it is unclear how far he distinguishes the two senses.[12] The criticism he offers, however, is straightforward. It is that in a syllogism such as 'Every man is an animal, and Socrates is a man, therefore Socrates is an animal', the universal proposition is arrived at by induction from particular propositions such as that which figures in the conclusion, so the truth of the former depends upon that of the latter; consequently those who then deduce the conclusion 'fall into the error of circular reasoning, since they are establishing the universal proposition inductively by means of each of the particulars and deducing the particular propositions from the universal syllogistically'.[13] The thrust of the argument is that it is circular to establish the truth of a universal proposition on the basis of the truth of particular propositions, and then to deduce the truth of the particular propositions from that of the universal proposition: the universal proposition simply plays no genuine role in such an argument. Of course, if our universal proposition is formed on the basis of an incomplete enumeration of instances, then the conclusion may be independent of the actual evidence for the universal proposition, but in that case the universal proposition will be 'disputed and non-evident', as Sextus puts it, so no demonstration will be possible, for the reason that we cannot demonstrate something from disputed premisses.

There are two questions at issue here: whether, as a result of deducing a conclusion from certain kinds of premiss, our cognitive

[12] *Outlines of Pyrrhonism*, II, §§ 193–4.
[13] *Outlines of Pyrrhonism*, II, § 196; Loeb edn., trans. Bury, i. 277–9.

grasp of that conclusion is different from the grasp we would have had if we had come by it in some other way; and whether the syllogism can in any sense be an instrument of discovery. These are different questions: Aristotle, for example, gives an affirmative answer to the first and a negative answer to the second. But they are also distinct from the sceptical question of whether the syllogism provides proofs. The sceptical question has as its concern the nature of deduction, and so affects all syllogisms—whether categorical or modal, dialectical or demonstrative—equally. The questions of cognitive circularity and discovery concern only the demonstrative syllogism, a special type of first-figure categorical syllogism. What Aristotle is concerned with in scientific demonstration is not universal propositions as such but 'commensurately universal' propositions, where there is a commensurately universal relation between a subject and an attribute when the attribute 'belongs to every instance of the subject essentially and as such, from which it follows that all commensurate universals inhere necessarily in their subjects' (*An. Post.* A4, 73^b 17–28). What is at issue here may become clearer if we compare the following syllogisms:

The planets do not twinkle

That which does not twinkle is near

The planets are near

The planets are near

That which is near does not twinkle

The planets do not twinkle

In Aristotle's discussion of these syllogisms (*An. Post.* A17, 78^a 13 ff.), he argues that the first is only a demonstration of fact (ὅτι), whereas the second is a demonstration of 'why' (διότι) or a scientific demonstration. In the latter, we are provided with a reason or cause or explanation (αἰτία) of the conclusion: the reason why the planets do not twinkle is that they are near. In the former, we have a valid but not demonstrative argument, since the planets' not twinkling is hardly a cause or explanation of their being near. So the first syllogism is in some way uninformative compared to the second, demonstrative or scientific syllogism: the latter produces understanding, the former does not (*An. Post. A*2, 71^b 24–5).

Aristotle maintains that we recognize the difference here by a form of intellectual insight which he calls νοῦς. But what exactly is the difference that we are supposed to recognize? It cannot consist in a difference in how the conclusions are deduced, for in our example both syllogisms are in the *Barbara* mode, so the conclusions must be deduced in exactly the same way. If Aristotelian syllogistic tells us anything it tells us this. Nor can the issue lie in the premisses stating something which is, for example, a physical cause of, or natural-philosophical explanation of, what is described in the conclusion, for this can be done using many kinds of syllogism, yet Aristotle is insistent that only those syllogisms which are perfect or complete (τέλειος)—that is, first-figure—and categorical can be demonstrative. So we must look elsewhere for a characterization of the difference, but where? There is a holist view of proof or demonstration according to which inference relations are meaning relations, so that a new proof of a proposition is to be seen in some way as providing it with a new meaning. Perhaps this captures some aspects of what Aristotle needs, but it must be ruled out because it would allow the conclusions of non-demonstrative syllogisms to be just as informative as those of demonstrative syllogisms. On the other hand, there are arguments where the premisses considered together tell us something we might not have realized had we considered the premisses separately, but such cases do not depend in any way upon a causal connection between premisses and conclusion, only upon our seeing a connection between the premisses. Consequently, it remains obscure what distinguishes the conclusions of demonstrative and non-demonstrative syllogisms. And while this is obscure, we have no protection against Sextus' charge of circularity.

In sum, if we leave to one side the question of discovery, which I have not looked at yet, we can distinguish two things that could be involved in the traditional criticism of the syllogism as a *petitio principii*. The first is a sceptical argument which denies that there is any such thing as proof. We can say in outline how this argument is to be met, namely by refusing to allow that all conditionals are automatically inferences. The second argument focuses upon syllogisms in which the kind of evidence which one would need to support one of the premises is that supplied by or presupposed by the conclusion, in which case the argument is circular. This objection is a perfectly legitimate one in the case of the demonstrative syllogism.

THE HEURISTIC ROLE OF THE SYLLOGISM

In Rule 10 of the *Regulae*, Descartes follows up his remark about syllogisms needing to have already ascertained the truth of what they purport to deduce, with a rejection of the syllogism as unproductive of truth:

Whence it is clear that they can gather nothing that is new [from the syllogism], and hence that dialectic as commonly understood is useless for those who desire to investigate the truth of things, and it can only serve to explain more easily the truths that we have already ascertained to others; hence it should be transferred from philosophy to rhetoric. (AT x. 406.)

The *Discourse on Method* contains much the same point:

I observed in respect to logic that its syllogisms and the greater part of its other teachings/rules served better in explaining to others those things that one knows, or like the art of Lull, in enabling one to speak without judgement of things of which one is ignorant, than in learning what is new. (AT vi. 17.)

In short, the syllogism cannot be an instrument of discovery, in the sense of the conclusion telling us something factually new.

Descartes is surely right here, but the point is so easily secured that one is tempted to wonder whether it rests on a misunderstanding of the function of the demonstrative syllogism. If we compare the two *Barbara* syllogisms above, one non-demonstrative and one demonstrative, with the parallel case in the Stoic account of demonstration, a rather interesting fact comes to light. The parallel case is this:

> If it is day, it is light
>
> It is day
> _____
>
> It is light

> If sweat flows through the skin, then there are invisible pores in the flesh
>
> Sweat flows through the skin
> _____
>
> There are invisible pores in the flesh

Again, there is no formal difference between these arguments, but the second is purportedly a scientific demonstration whereas the first is not. The reason, it is maintained, is that in the second the conclusion is not evident independently of the argument, whereas in the first it is. In the scientific argument, the premisses are evident: the conditional premiss is said to be rationally self-evident (it is really the result of an inference to the best explanation), the minor premiss is empirically self-evident. So we deduce a non-evident conclusion from self-evident premisses.[14] Now one might quarrel with the claim that the conditional premiss is self-evident and the conclusion non-evident. It is not too difficult to see how one might argue that the kinds of consideration that might lead one to consider the conditional premiss self-evident would be the same as those that might lead one to consider the conclusion

[14] On Stoic demonstration cf. B. Mates, *Stoic Logic* (Berkeley, 1961); W. and M. Kneale, *The Development of Logic* (Oxford, 1962), ch. 3; J. Gould, 'Deduction in Stoic Logic', and J. Corcoran, 'Remarks on Stoic Deduction', both in J. Corcoran (ed.), *Ancient Logic and its Modern Interpretations* (Dordrecht, 1974); J. Brunschwig, 'Proof Defined', in Schofield, Burnyeat, and Barnes, *Doubt and Dogmatism*, 125–60.

self-evident. Consequently, it is not difficult to see how the circularity argument could be brought against Stoic forms of demonstration. But this would have to be argued. There is at least a prima-facie basis for a claim, whether it can ultimately be defended or not, that the conclusion tells us something factually new. Such a prima-facie basis is conspicuously lacking in the Aristotelian case: the conclusion does not have the slightest appearance of being a factual discovery.

This is not as surprising as it may seem. The demonstrative syllogism was designed not as a research tool but as a purely expository and didactic device. This was shown definitively nearly twenty years ago by Jonathan Barnes,[15] although a number of commentators, beginning with Grote and Maier at the end of the nineteenth century, have suggested as much. In the light of this, we would expect the principal qualities of the demonstrative syllogism to be pedagogic, such as its being an economical conveyer of information and being easily memorized, rather than those which might enable a practising scientist to conduct research. And indeed the merits of the demonstrative syllogism fall squarely within the former area, and are virtually non-existent in the latter. This is not to say that none of Aristotle's followers took the demonstrative syllogism to be a means of advancing knowledge rather than just formalizing it. But it is instructive that those who, like Galen, did construe it in this way, took it as a means for discovering middle terms, not as a means of discovering novel conclusions. Whether one takes the strict Aristotelian or the Galenic view, the object is not to find novel conclusions, but to find the middle terms which enable one to draw a necessary and universal connection between premisses and conclusion. Now the finding of middle terms is not the task of syllogistic for Aristotle, and this is where the strict Aristotelian differs from the Galenic view. Aristotle attempts to discover middle terms through the topics. The role of the topics is to provide devices or strategies for

---

[15] J. Barnes, 'Aristotle's Theory of Demonstration', in J. Barnes, M. Schofield, and R. Sorabji (eds.), *Articles on Aristotle*, i: *Science* (London, 1975), 65–87. This is a revised version of a paper that originally appeared in *Phronesis* in 1969.

classifying or characterizing problems so that they can be solved using set techniques. They provide the distinctions needed if we are to be able to formulate problems properly, as well as supplying devices which enable us to determine what has to be shown if the conclusion we want to arrive at is to be achieved. The home ground of the topics is dialectic, where they function as a rather more sophisticated and profound version of the Sophists' devices for disputation. They also have a place in rhetoric. But they play a role in science as well, and here such devices are designed to take us, ultimately, to first principles which can be grasped in their own right by some form of immediate intellectual apprehension ($\nu o\hat{u}s$). Aristotle begins his scientific texts not with a presentation of first principles but with a dialectical discussion of the views of his predecessors and contemporaries. As Weil has put it, the topics, 'working from a historically given state of human knowledge, enable us to formulate the questions that have to be posed and to discover those true theses on which formally valid demonstration can found a useful and lasting science'.[16]

So it is the topics that play the role of a method of discovery in Aristotle. Descartes was, of course, familiar with the topics, which generated an industry second to none in later antiquity and the Middle Ages, and received a new lease of life in the hands of Ramus in the sixteenth century.[17] But Descartes's view of the topics is as critical as his view of the syllogism, and indeed mirrors his criticism of the syllogism to such an extent that it is difficult to avoid the conclusion that he considered them simply two inseparable aspects of the one misguided enterprise. Here is his criticism of the Porphyrian tree[18] in the *Search after Truth*:

[16] E. Weil, 'The Place of Logic in Aristotle's Thought', in Barnes, Schofield, and Sorabji, *Articles on Aristotle*, i. 94; cf. also G. E. L. Owen, 'Tithenai ta phainomena' in the same collection, 113–26.

[17] Cf. E. R. Curtius, *European Literature and the Latin Middle Ages* (Princeton, 1973), M. Fumaroli, *L'Âge de l'éloquence* (Geneva, 1980), and W. J. Ong, *Ramus, Method, and the Decay of Dialogue* (Cambridge, Mass., 1958).

[18] The Porphyrian tree is a device whereby we proceed by means of dichotomous division from substance, through body, animate body, animal, rational animal, to mortal rational animal. This system of division played an important role in the medieval doctrine of predicables. It originates as a logical device in Boethius, but the basic suggestion of the tree derives from Porphyry's *Isagoge*.

Were I for example to ask Epistemon himself what a man is, and were he to reply, as is done in the Schools, that a man is a rational animal, and if, in addition, in order to explain these two terms which are no less obscure than the first, he conducted us by all the steps which are termed metaphysical, we should be dragged into a maze from which we would never be able to emerge. For from this question two others arise: the first is what is an animal?, the second, what is rational? And further, if in order to explain what an animal is he were to reply that it is a living thing which has sensations, that a living thing is an animate body, and that a body is a corporeal substance, you see that the questions would go on increasing and multiplying like the branches of a genealogical tree; and finally all these wonderful questions would finish in pure tautology, which would clear up nothing, and would leave us in our original ignorance. (AT x. 515–16.)

It would be easy to treat Descartes's incomprehension here as feigned. There is rhetorical overkill, but there is also a real element in his failure to understand how topical reasoning could lead anywhere. It is not easy for us to share his incomprehension in the case of Aristotle. Aristotle's topics seem a not wholly implausible way of going about formulating genuine scientific questions and first principles: they are designed to provide us with some guidance, based upon consideration of earlier and contemporary views on the subject-matter at issue, as to what are going to be the most fruitful questions to pose. But Descartes, in his mention of the Schools and the Porphyrian tree—which forms the backbone of medieval accounts of the topics—indicates that he does not have Aristotle's account in mind, but rather the medieval accounts of the topics. In this context, it is understandable that Descartes should wish to transfer study of the topics to rhetoric, for by the later Middle Ages the relevance of the topics to scientific discovery had become very obscure, and it is usually Cicero and Quintilian who provide the models, not Aristotle. And these models are rhetorical. Consequently, it is not surprising that when, in the sixteenth century, Zabarella, Pacius, Schegk, and others finally begin to clarify the distinction between methods of investigation and methods of presentation, it is to the Galenic model, which makes no reference to the topics, that they turn.[19]

The problem is not a wholly medieval one, however, for in one very important respect it goes back to Aristotle himself. Between the early Books II to VII of the *Topics*, on the one hand, and the mature *Analytics*, on the other, there is a shift from concern with questions of discovery towards a concern with questions of presenting already achieved results. This shift requires some explanation, although it is not concerned with the latter as such that causes the problem: education ($\pi\alpha\iota\delta\epsilon\iota\alpha$) had traditionally played a central role in Greek philosophy, and indeed Jaeger has argued persuasively that classical philosophy was born from the Socratic problem of whether $\pi\alpha\iota\delta\epsilon\iota\alpha$ is possible.[20] But within a scientific context, it is at first puzzling that Aristotle should apparently come to think that imparting knowledge was more worthy of attention than the discovery of new knowledge. The fact is, however, that there is some evidence that Aristotle thought that the vast bulk of what there was to be known was already known, so the pressing task was to co-ordinate this knowledge and present it in a systematic and economic fashion.[21] Unfortunately we cannot ascertain Aristotle's commitment to the 'end of science' view with any great degree of certainty. His medieval and Renaissance successors, on the other hand, whether sympathetic or hostile to Aristotle, certainly took this view. As late as the seventeenth century we can find a flourishing Aristotelian 'textbook' tradition.[22] And the humanist opponents of Artistotelianism took an even stronger view: for many of them science actually had come to an end in antiquity. Ramus, for example, construes knowledge in completely pedagogic terms, transforming the topics into a system

---

[19] For a general account of these developments cf. J. H. Randall, *The School of Padua and the Emergence of Modern Science* (Padua, 1961) and N. W. Gilbert, *Renaissance Concepts of Method* (New York, 1960).

[20] W. Jaeger, *Paideia* (3 vols., Oxford, 1939–45), vol. ii.

[21] Cf. J. Barnes, 'Aristotle's Theory of Demonstration', pp. 85–6.

[22] Cf. P. Reif, 'The Textbook Tradition in Natural Philosophy, 1600–1650', *Journal of the History of Ideas*, 30 (1969), 17–32.

of pedagogic classification of knowledge, where the point of the exercise is to enable us to refer any question back to the storehouse of ancient wisdom, the purpose of the topics being to provide us with points of entry into this storehouse.

There is a deep and genuine problem here which we must grasp if we are to be able to appreciate the psychological and polemical strength of Descartes's rejection of the syllogism as circular and unproductive of new truths. It is not just that what, for Aristotle, is a method of presentation is mistaken for a method of discovery, but that the method of discovery becomes in some way lost or unrecognizable. Despite the attempts of the *regressus* theorists of the sixteenth century to reconstruct the method of discovery along what were essentially Galenic lines, the simple fact is that from the Middle Ages onwards the results of Aristotelian science have for all intents and purposes lost all contact with the procedures of discovery which produced them. While these results remained unchallenged, the problem was not particularly apparent. But when they came to be challenged in a serious and systematic way, as they were from the sixteenth century onwards, they began to take on the appearance of mere dogmas, backed up by circular reasoning.

One casualty of this challenge was the conception of deductive inference encapsulated in syllogistic reasoning and the rules governing that reasoning. Part of the problem here, as I have indicated, lay in the conflation of a sceptical argument denying the existence of proof, with an argument showing that the deduction of the truth of a conclusion from premises in cases where the evidence for the premises is provided or presupposed by the conclusion is circular. We can now see that the problem is further complicated by the fact that forms of argument designed to systematize results are taken to be forms of argument designed to reveal those results. There is no way in which the syllogism can plausibly be said to advance knowledge in the sense of revealing new factual information to us. Yet there was a medieval and to some extent classical precedent for interpreting it in this way, and the challenge to syllogistic was an important part of the challenge to traditional natural philosophy in the sixteenth and seventeenth centuries. The upshot was that, just as one was faced with a choice between traditional natural philosophy and the new astronomical and physical theories of Kepler, Galileo, and others, so too was one faced with an associated choice between syllogistic and a new method of discovery.

The problem goes even deeper than this, however, for whatever the merits of syllogistic as a method of discovery, it had provided something much more fundamental than this in antiquity and the Middle Ages, namely, a model of reasoning or, more generally, cognitive grasp. A method of discovery in itself could not provide such a model. But some account of cognitive grasp was needed. Because of the running together of the various issues that I have attempted to delineate in this chapter, syllogistic, in being discredited as a method of discovery, was generally discredited, so could no longer provide a general model of cognitive grasp. Something else had therefore to provide this model. This will be our concern in the next chapter.

2

Descartes's Conception of Inference

THE argument against syllogistic that Descartes pursues with most vigour is not one which turns on its circularity or unsuitability as a method of discovery, but rather one that shows it to be an impediment to the conduct of our reasoning. This is a completely different kind of argument from those that we have discussed up to now. In Rule 4 of the *Regulae*, we are told:

But if our method rightly explains how intellectual intuition should be used, so as not to fall into error contrary to truth, and how one must find deductive paths so that we may arrive at knowledge of all things, I cannot see anything else is needed to make it complete; for I have already said that the only way science is to be acquired is by intellectual intuition or by deduction. Method cannot be extended further so as to show how these operations themselves should be effected, because they are the most simple and primary of all, to the extent that, unless our understanding were already able to make use of them, it could comprehend none of the precepts of that very method, not even the simplest. As for the other operations of the mind, which dialectic claims to direct by making use of these two, they are quite useless here; rather they are to be accounted impediments, because nothing can be added to the pure light of reason which does not in some way obscure it. (AT x. 372–3.)

This 'light of reason', or 'light of nature' as it is called in Rule 10, apparently cannot mislead us, as 'none of the mistakes which men make . . . are due to faulty inference; they are caused merely by the fact that we build upon the basis of poorly comprehended experiences, or because hasty or groundless propositions are put forward' (AT x. 365).

What the light of reason does in the first instance is to allow us to grasp the truth of clear and distinct ideas. But of course on some occasions we have to connect such ideas inferentially, and then we require demonstration or deduction. Descartes's account of this process is, however, modelled upon intellectual intuition (*intuitus*):

Thus if, for example, I have first found out, by distinct mental operations, what relation exists between the magnitudes *A* and *B*, then what between *B* and *C*, between *C* and *D*, and finally between *D* and *E*, that does not entail that I will see what the relation is between *A* and *E*, nor can the truths previously learned give me a precise idea of it unless I recall them all. To remedy this I would run over them many times, by a continuous movement of the imagination, in such a way that it has an intuition of each term at the same time that it passes on to the others, and this I would do until I learned to pass from the first relation to the last so quickly that there was almost no role left for memory and I seemed to have the whole before me at the same time. (AT x. 521.)

One way in which this passage has been taken is as a claim that deduction has no real role to play in knowledge. Ian Hacking takes it in such a way, assimilating Descartes's view to that of the mathematician G. H. Hardy, who thought of proofs as 'gas, rhetorical flourishes designed to affect psychology . . . devices to stimulate the imagination of pupils'.[1]

Hacking supports his reading by appeal to the doctrine of eternal truths. This doctrine, first elaborated in three letters to Mersenne of 15 April, 6 May, and 27 May 1630, offers an account of God's grasp of truths. The second letter presents the essentials of the doctrine:

As for the eternal truths, I say once again that *they are true or possible only because God knows them as true or possible and are not known as true by God in such a way as would imply that they are true independently of Him.* If men really understood the meaning of their words they would never be able to say without blasphemy that the truth of anything is prior to the knowledge which God has of it, for in God willing and knowing are a

[1] I. Hacking, 'Proof and Eternal Truths: Descartes and Leibniz', in S. Gaukroger (ed.), *Descartes* (Sussex, 1980), 169–80. Hacking's interpretation is indebted to Y. Belaval, *Leibniz: Critique de Descartes* (Paris, 1960).

single thing so that *by the very fact of willing something He knows it and it is only for this reason that such a thing is true.* (AT i. 149.)[2]

The central claim is elaborated upon in the third letter in these terms:

> You ask what necessitated God to create these truths: to which I say that He was no less free to make it untrue that all the lines drawn from the centre of a circle to its circumference are equal, than He was not to create the world. And it is certain that these truths are no more necessarily attached to His essence than other creations are. You ask what God did to produce them. I reply that *from all eternity He willed and understood them to be, and by that very fact He created them.* In God, willing, understanding, and creating are all the same thing without the one being prior to the other even *conceptually.* (AT i. 152–3.)

Hacking takes the doctrine of intuition and the doctrine of eternal truths together as illustrations of an underlying conception of the irrelevance of proof to truth. Construed in this context, the import of the doctrine of eternal truths is that eternal truths depend upon the will of God, who has no need of deduction (proof); he knows truths in virtue of having created them (i.e. willed them), so proof is clearly irrelevant. This doctrine then seems to mirror the doctrine of intuition which, on Hacking's interpretation, maintains that we need only intuition, and not deduction, in grasping truths.

There are a number of problems with this association of the two doctrines. In the first place, they are developed independently. The earliest appearance of the doctrine of intuition is Rule 3 of the *Regulae*, which dates from around 1619.[3] The doctrine of eternal truths, on the other hand, only makes an appearance in 1630, in the letters to Mersenne. Moreover, although the term *intuitus* tends to disappear after the *Regulae*, the doctrine itself does not— it is to be found as late as the 1640s in the *Search after Truth* (AT x. 521),[4] for example—yet this doctrine is not altered after 1630 in

---

[2] In this, as in the next quotation, words in italics designate Latin phrases.

[3] On the question of dating cf. J.-P. Weber, *La Constitution du texte des Regulae* (Paris, 1964).

[4] This is a passage that I shall return to below. On the dating of the *Search after Truth* see F. Alquié (ed.), *Descartes: Œuvres philosophiques* (3 vols., Paris, 1963–73), ii. 1101–4.

any way which would suggest that it had a connection with the new conception of eternal truths. Secondly, while Descartes holds both doctrines after 1630, he *never* discusses them together or even in the same context. As well as the three letters to Mersenne of 1630, the doctrine of eternal truths is discussed or mentioned in letters to Mersenne of 17 May 1638 and to Mesland of 2 May 1644, in the *Replies to the Fifth and Sixth sets of Objections to the Meditations* and in the *Principles* (I, arts. 22–4 and 48–9). It is hard to believe that, if the doctrines were simply part of the one underlying conception, Descartes would have made no effort to discuss them together or indeed to make any explicit connection between them. Third, not only is there no textual reason to associate the doctrines in the way that Hacking suggests, there are other grounds for believing such an association to be mistaken. Hacking points out that Leibniz's God knows all truths because he knows all proofs, whereas we only know some because we only know some proofs, and we are in any case restricted in our grasp of proofs to those which are finite whereas God is not. But what is the parallel with Descartes here? Consider the doctrine of intuition. The parallel that suggests itself on the basis of this conception is one on which God has an intuitive grasp of all truths, but we only have an intuitive grasp of a few. We would then be able to conclude, as Hacking does, that, in general terms, proof is constitutive of truth for Leibniz and irrelevant to truth for Descartes. But the whole thrust of the doctrine of eternal truths is precisely that we *cannot* compare what knowledge for us consists in and what knowledge for God consists in. We are simply unable, on Descartes's view, to make any connection at all between our intuition and God's cognitive grasp.

In discussing the doctrine of eternal truths, Descartes never raises the question of deduction or proof, and this is the crucial point. He nowhere maintains that proof is irrelevant to truth for God. He does provide us with an account whereby God wills truths into existence, an account which, if construed in a logical context, does indeed have this as a consequence. But it is far from clear that Descartes thinks such questions can be construed in a logical context, since it appears that we can say nothing at all about what God's grasp of truth consists in. Hence, if we are to understand the conception of inference that Descartes offers, we must focus our attention on what I have called the doctrine of intuition.

On the face of it, this is not a particularly attractive doctrine, and even if we dissociate it from the doctrine of eternal truths, it has two features which may appear to lend support to Hacking's low view of Descartes's general conception of inference. First, in the limiting case, deduction tends towards what is in effect the model for all reasoning, intuition. The point of the exercise seems to be to reduce out inferential steps altogether, so that one grasps the premisses and conclusion in the one intuition. The role of demonstration or proof on this conception is obviously problematic. Secondly, for Descartes, knowledge which we have in an intuition is an immediate grasp of clear and distinct ideas which Descartes construes explicitly as thoughts, thoughts which are grasped in the first instance in their own right without any reference to whatever extra-mental correlates they may have. So not only is deduction construed (in some way that we have yet to elucidate) in terms of intuition, but intuition, and hence deduction, is construed psychologistically. Psychologism has not generally been taken seriously as a basis for logic since Frege's famous attack on it,[5] and its faults now seem as obvious to us as the faults of syllogistic seemed to Descartes.[6] What we need to come to terms with in understanding Descartes is not just his psychologism, however, but more importantly the issues that underlie his advocacy of psychologism. Psychologism is simply the form taken by Descartes's attempt to provide what, I shall argue, is a cognitive basis for inference. To appreciate what is at issue here we need to take a broad view of the development of conceptions of inference up to Descartes's time. I shall look first briefly at Aristotle's conception of inference, and at how the Aristotelian conception comes to be transformed in the early Middle Ages, and then at the

---

[5] G. Frege, *The Foundations of Arithmetic* (Oxford, 1959), §§26–7.
[6] But cf. B. Ellis, *Rational Belief Systems* (Oxford, 1979).

views of Descartes's immediate predecessors and contemporaries. Although this means ignoring the very important Stoic and Terminist conceptions of logic, as well as many other less important theories, I believe the selection provides us with a broad outline of the central development, which I shall argue lies in a shift from discursive to facultative conceptions of inference. Seen in this light, Descartes is the first to make a serious attempt to come to terms with a novel and important but especially intractable problem about the cognitive basis of inference.

CONCEPTIONS OF LOGIC BEFORE DESCARTES

Aristotelian syllogistic was misunderstood in many respects in the seventeenth century, by both its detractors and its ever-decreasing number of advocates. The charges of circularity and question-begging which were levelled against the syllogism, for instance by Descartes and Locke, depended to a large extent upon its being taken as an instrument of discovery, which, as we have seen, is something that Aristotle never intended. For Aristotle, the demonstrative syllogism in particular was primarily a didactic and expository device which provided an explanation of a conclusion which was known in advance. The procedure for yielding such conclusions was provided not by syllogistic, the concern of which was formal and systematic presentation, but by the topics. As we have seen, the topics work by supplying strategies for classifying or characterizing problems in such a way that they can be solved using set techniques of argument or disputation which are initially developed in the context of dialectical argument, where they function somewhat like the Sophists' procedures, and which help one to discover what distinctions are to be made, what route is to be followed, and so on, if one is to get one's opponent to yield to the case one is defending. But as Aristotle becomes progressively more concerned with the formal properties of arguments and with scientific demonstration, the topics come to be supplemented by a formal account of the structure of arguments: syllogistic. They

retain their role as an instrument of discovery, but are superseded
in many other respects by syllogistic.

The pioneering work of Łukasiewicz[7] and others showing, from
the perspective of modern logic, the formidable formal strengths
of Aristotelian syllogistic, has tended to open up a gulf between the
early dialectical concerns of the central Books II to VII of the
Topics and the concerns of the mature *Analytics*, and this shift of
interest is very easily seen as a shift from a concern with discursive
reasoning to a concern with 'pure' patterns of inference. But
Aristotle's syllogistic grows out of the dialectic of the *Topics* and
the *De sophisticis elenchis*, and it retains important traces of its
dialectical origins. Kapp has given a particularly insightful account
of this discursive context of syllogistic reasoning in his now classic
article on syllogistic in Pauly–Wissowa's *Real-Encyclopädie*.[8]
Kapp's argument is that the syllogism should be seen as a real
process in which two people participate. We have already noted
that the conclusions of Aristotelian syllogisms are not sought but
are given before the construction of the syllogism. What is sought
is the premisses which will yield those conclusions in the requisite
way. The path to be followed in such a search is clearly the reverse
of syllogistic inference. If, following Kapp, we let *A* seek the
premisses, then upon finding them by this reverse path *A* is in a
position to construct a syllogism, and to present this syllogism to
B who, in grasping that syllogism, moves inferentially from
premisses to conclusion. The process described in Aristotle's
definition of the syllogism—namely, that certain things (the
premisses) being stated, something other than what is stated (the
conclusion) follows of necessity from the truth of those things
alone (*An. Pr. A*1, 24^b 18–22)—occurs as an intellectual process
in *B*. But the syllogism itself is not to be identified with *B*'s mental
activity: *A* and not *B* is responsible for the syllogism which *B*
grasps. That syllogism is therefore in an important sense independent of *B*, who can only accept or reject it. In other words, the

[7] J. Łukasiewicz, *Aristotle's Syllogistic* (Oxford, 1957).

[8] Translated into English as 'Syllogistic', in J. Barnes, M. Schofield, and R. Sorabji
(eds.), *Articles on Aristotle*, i: *Science* (London, 1975), 35–49.

context of syllogistic is a thoroughly discursive one. This is true not only of paradigmatic case of the dialectical syllogism—where A and B are opponents, and where the point of the exercise is for A, by employing dialectical skills, to get B to accept something contentious—but equally so of the demonstrative syllogism, where A and B are teacher and pupil respectively, the point of the exercise now being for A to convey information to B in the most effective and economic way.

The fact that it is the topics that provide the discursive model for syllogistic is interesting in the light of their subsequent history. The topics underwent a number of changes after Aristotle, with Themistius and Cicero providing their own systems of topics, and Boethius providing what was to be the definitive system of antiquity as far as the Middle Ages was concerned. Yet while there is on the face of it a fundamental gulf separating Aristotle and Boethius—their lists of topics differ considerably and are organized in different ways, as well as offering different procedures by which to find arguments by means of these topics[9]—there is one crucial question on which they are in agreement, and which distinguishes the topical systems of antiquity from those of the Middle Ages. The topics were above all dialectical in antiquity. They are explicitly concerned with the art of disputation in Aristotle, and this concern is retained throughout antiquity. Boethius' account of the topics, for example, is firmly within the context of arguing by question and answer, and in developing arguments for and encouraging belief in conclusions. There is a stark contrast between this and the medieval approach. The difference is apparent in the very earliest extant medieval logical text—Garlandus Compotista's *Dialectica*, composed probably in the early eleventh century—where the focus is not upon the discovery of arguments but upon their confirmation, with a special emphasis on enthymemes.[10] The context of disputation is merely

[9] Cf. E. Stump, *Boethius' De topicis differentiis* (Ithaca, 1978), 159–261, on the changes in the topics in antiquity and the early Middle Ages. On the development of the use of the topics in rhetoric in this period see E. R. Curtius, *European Literature and the Latin Middle Ages* (Princeton, 1973).

[10] See E. Stump, 'Garlandus Compotista and Dialectic in the Eleventh and Twelfth Centuries', *History and Philosophy of Logic*, 1 (1980), 1–18.

perfunctory, as indeed it is also in the case of the standard medieval account of the topics, that provided two centuries later by Peter of Spain in his *Tractatus*. Peter does not conceive of the topics in terms of questions or of inducing one's opponents to believe something, but rather in terms of supplying explanations and justifications of correct but enthymematic inferences.[11]

Peter of Spain's work lies at the heart of subsequent developments in logic up to Descartes, and the two most influential conceptions of logic in the sixteenth and early seventeenth centuries can be distinguished in terms of the attitude that they take to Peter of Spain. The humanist view, which in this period takes the form of Ramism, takes its starting-point from Agricola's rejection of Peter's conception of logic. The scholastic view of logic, on the other hand, which in this period principally takes the form of the Jesuit theory of *directio ingenii* or 'directions for thinking', is a development, albeit a considerably revised one, of Peter's account. These are not the only views which flourished in the period but *regressus* theory, for example, had no influence in the seventeenth century, and little outside Padua in the sixteenth century, and the only other influential school—the so-called 'systematics' (Keckermann, Buscherus, Libavius, Alsted, and Timpler)[12]—were concerned to reform scholastic logic in the light of Ramist criticisms, so need no separate attention here.

The humanist interpretation of logic has two landmarks which deserve our attention: Rudolph Agricola's *De inventione dialectica libri tres*, first published in 1515 but circulated in manuscript form from the 1480s, and the writings of Peter Ramus, and his collaborator Omar Talon, from the 1540s onwards. The *De inventione dialectica*, although undeniably indebted to earlier humanist writings, was virtually synonymous with logic or dialectic in the first part of the sixteenth century, and with the derivative works of Melanchthon and Caesarius it quickly replaced Peter of

[11] Cf. Stump, *Boethius' De topicis*, pp. 235–6.

[12] On the 'Systematics' see W. S. Howell, *Logic and Rhetoric in England, 1500–1700* (Princeton, 1956) and W. Risse, *Die Logik der Neuzeit*, i: *1500–1640* (Stuttgart and Bad Cannstatt, 1964).

Spain and Paul of Venice as the standard textbook on dialectic, being overshadowed in the later sixteenth century only by Ramus' work, which owes a great deal to Agricola. Logic or dialectic must be understood broadly here. As a component of the *trivium*, dialectic was theoretically an equal partner with grammar and rhetoric, but it was usually defined in such broad terms that it overshadowed the other two. Peter of Spain and Lambert of Auxerre, enlarging on the Aristotelian definition (*Top. A*2, 101^b 3), define it as 'the art of arts, the science of sciences, possessing the path to the principles of all methods'. Agricola's conception of dialectic is a development of Peter of Spain's[13] and it involves dialectic taking over everything except actual delivery from rhetoric, which in turn is reduced to ornamentation. Parallel with this there is what can only be called a homogenization of dialectic. Aristotle had distinguished between various forms of syllogism— dialectical, eristic, demonstrative—and had conceived of discourse being directed towards scientific, dialectical, rhetorical, and other ends, and Aquinas had elaborated upon the different forms of argumentation and the different ends of discourse. But as far as scholastic thinking about dialectic was concerned, it was Peter of Spain's broad conception, not that of Aristotle or Aquinas, that held sway, and the humanists capitalized on this broad undifferentiated conception. For Agricola, all dialectic, which now effectively comprises a general theory of discourse, has a single aim, and that aim is teaching. Cicero had distinguished teaching, moving, and pleasing as the three objectives of discourse (*Opt. Gen.* II), but Agricola points out that we can teach without moving or pleasing but not vice versa (*De inv. dial.* Bk. I, ch. i), and concludes that teaching is the only universal and intrinsic function of speech (Bk. II, ch. iv). There is no shortage of precedent in antiquity for this view. The later Stoics, for example, held firmly to the view that the function of literature is pre-eminently didactic, and Seneca and

---

[13] Cf. W. J. Ong, *Ramus, Method, and the Decay of Dialogue* (Cambridge, Mass., 1958), chs. 4 and 5.

others developed a mimetic theory of literature and poetry on this basis.[14]

On Agricola's account, whether our immediate ends are rhetorical or scientific or whatever, we are always ultimately engaged in teaching. Indeed, one looks in vain for the logic of discovery or 'invention' mentioned in the title of Agricola's work: the whole purpose of logic or dialectic is the ordering of material so as to convey it to an audience. Ramus draws on this conception and gives the topics the central role of sorting ideas into appropriate groups, but the topics in turn are conceived in a completely pedagogic fashion. The structure of knowledge is dictated in Ramus by the pedagogic classification of the arts and sciences; as Ong puts it, 'Ramus assumes that the primary units which the mind "contains" are the objects in the curriculum',[15] that is the curriculum subjects. In this respect, Ramism can be seen as an extreme version of Aristotle's mature preoccupation with the question of organizing and presenting already attained knowledge, an attitude reinforced in both cases by a belief that learning is virtually complete and remains only to be recovered and conveyed. That much of this learning had become lost and needed rediscovering was a prominent theme in writers such as Ramus and Melanchthon. Moreover, once the learning had been recovered, it was a question not merely of presenting it, but of presenting it persuasively, and this itself was a topic to which much attention had to be devoted.[16] It remains the case, nevertheless, that what is centrally at issue is the presentation of something that had been known in antiquity, and there was no question of discovering something which had never been known. Indeed, in his earlier writings, Ramus' thinking has an explicitly Platonist ingredient, whereby ideas in the mind are prior to the empirical world,

---

[14] Cf. M. L. Colish, *The Stoic Tradition from Antiquity to the Early Middle Ages* (2 vols., Leiden, 1985), i: 56–60.

[15] Ong, *Ramus*, p. 197.

[16] On themes cf. M. Fumaroli, *L'Âge de l'éloquence* (Geneva, 1980) and C. Vasoli, *La dialettica e la retorica dell'umanesimo: Invenzione e metodo nella cultura del XV–XVI secolo* (Milan, 1968).

and there is even a hint of the Platonic doctrine of recollection.[17]
There is no role for demonstration, if by this we mean logical
inference, on this conception. The 'principles of the arts', Ramus
tells us, 'are definitions and divisions; outside of these, nothing': to
'demonstrate' something is simply to define it.[18] Even geometry,
on Ramus' view, consists not of demonstrations properly speaking
but of definitions and rules. Because Ramus treats knowledge in
terms of mapping ideas accurately according to their definitions in
the mind, his treatment of reason effectively reduces it to the
operation of memory and classification, and the problem of
'method' and that of memory and classification become identical.
There had been a very active medieval concern with memory
which continued to flourish in the sixteenth century, according to
which the topics were construed in terms of places (*loci*, the Latin
translation of the Greek τόποι) in the mind where ideas were to be
found by employing mnemonic devices displaying the structure of
those places.[19] But this is too arbitrary for Ramus, because the
mnemonic systems, which typically worked with an image of a city
or a building intimately known to the subject, so that items in that
city or building could be associated with items of knowledge, need
in no way reflect the pedagogic ordering of knowledge. It is also
too complex for him, and, taking his cue from Quintilian, he
abolishes the *loci* and images and replaces them with the division
and definition of one's subject-matter.[20]

In sum, there are three elements in the humanist reformulation
of logic or dialectic. The first is the extension of the scope of
dialectic to cover everything except actual delivery and grammar,
thereby transforming what in antiquity was a theory of inference
into a general theory of discourse. In Ramus, this general theory of
discourse, guided by the all-encompassing 'method' that it

---

[17] The first (1543) version of the *Dialecticae institutiones* has explicitly Platonist elements,
which are discarded from the second (1546) version onwards. On the development of
Ramus' doctrines, cf. Ong, *Ramus*, chs. 8–12.

[18] *Arist. anim.* (1543), fos. 58 and 60. Cited in Ong, *Ramus*, p. 188.

[19] Cf. F. A. Yates, *The Art of Memory* (Harmondsworth, 1978).

[20] Cf. P. Rossi, *Clavis universalis* (Milan and Naples, 1960), 135 ff., esp. p. 140; also
Yates, *The Art of Memory*, ch. 10. Division and definition are versions of the Platonic
procedures of διαίρεσις and ὁρισμός.

employs, covers without distinction geometry, natural philosophy, poetry, military strategy, biography, and so on.[21] The second is the gradual destruction of the differentiations within logic, so that the distinctions between probabilistic and conclusive inference, inferences designed to convince opponents and those designed to convince pupils, inferences directed towards practical ends and those directed towards knowledge, all of these distinctions tend to become obliterated, and dialectic tends to be construed in terms of a single aim: teaching. Thirdly, the space traditionally occupied by inference now comes to be occupied by classificatory and mnemonic devices, as knowledge comes to be conceived in a thoroughly pedagogic fashion. Once we conceive of proof as a means of getting others to grasp what we already know, the move to conceiving of dialectic in purely pedagogic terms is a natural one. The point of the exercise is then to be able to reconstruct and find one's way around an already constituted body of knowledge, and for this one needs to be familiar with the structure (i.e. classification) of knowledge. Then, when we are faced with a new problem—in natural philosophy, geometry, public speaking, military strategy, metaphysics, or whatever—we can establish a connection between that problem and the storehouse of ancient wisdom which we have access to via the procedures of division and definition, which replace the cumbersome old mnemonic devices. Such procedures effectively take the place of syllogistic in that they lead us to knowledge. They are aids to knowledge and are in no way constitutive of knowledge, just as syllogistic was conceived in the Middle Ages and Renaissance as an aid to knowledge, albeit an unsuccessful one on the humanist view, and therefore to be replaced by something more efficient.

CONCEPTIONS OF COGNITIVE GRASP BEFORE
DESCARTES

It is crucial that we understand this conception of logic as an aid to knowledge if we are to appreciate how the humanists could

[21] See Ong, *Ramus*, p. 30.

conceive of replacing the Aristotelian *organon* with classificatory and mnemonic schemes. The idea of the *organon* providing an aid to knowledge is not one peculiar to the humanists, and it is premissed on an assumption widely held in the Middle Ages and Renaissance: that reasoning is the exercise of one's faculties, and that logic and inference have to be understood in terms of the mode of operation of those faculties. The question turns on the traditional distinction between the incorporeal intellect, and powers such as imagination (*phantasia*), reason (*cogitatio*), and memory (*memoria*), which were associated with the functioning of specific localized corporeal organs. There were two issues in dispute here from late antiquity onwards: (1) whether these corporeal faculties exhausted the workings of the mind or whether there was also an incorporeal intellect, and (2), if there were such an intellect, what its relation to the corporeal faculties was. We can distinguish three broad categories of reply to these questions. The first is naturalism, which allows only an embodied intellect. The second we can call transcendentalism; it holds that there is a complete separation between the intellect and the corporeal faculties. The third attempts to compromise between these two, and the most coherent such attempt was Aquinas's doctrine of analogy.

The problem derives in large part from Aristotle. Both Plato and Aristotle had taken the problem of accounting for change as one of their central concerns, and each had formulated a response to the Parmenidean denial of the existence of, and intelligibility of, change. Plato had postulated a transcendent realm of unchanging Forms beyond the sensible realm of nature: accepting Parmenides' dictum that what changed was unknowable, he argued that the real objects of knowledge are Forms, of which the sensible world is merely an imperfect reflection. Aristotle, gradually rejecting his erstwhile Platonism, came to argue that forms do not constitute a realm separate from that of the sensible world, but rather underlie the sensible world: they inhere in matter rather than inhabiting a realm that transcends that of matter. But Aristotle offers different accounts of this doctrine at different places, and even his terminology reflects two different conceptions. His discussion of change, for example, is sometimes couched in the vocabulary of the form (εἶδος), and sometimes in the vocabulary of 'actuality' (ἐνέργεια). In the former case, it is hard to avoid thinking of the forms as being somewhat like Plato's unchanging Forms: they are essentially principles of structure imposed on matter. In the latter case, however, we are presented with a much more organic conception of an essentially active internal principle directing what occurs in substances. Moreover, while Aristotle does occasionally consider the soul to be (at least in part) immortal and separable from the body, this view is at odds with his more usual conception of the soul in terms of a functional organizing principle of the body, and with his view that the soul is the form of the body, since he insists in a wide range of contexts that forms are always forms *of* something.

This latter conception was that stressed by Aristotle's successors in the Lyceum, but it was the Stoics who most thoroughly rid Aristotelianism of any dependence on transcendent forms. The Stoic doctrine of *pneuma* appears to have been largely taken over from Aristotle's account of how the *pneuma*, which is carried in the seminal fluid, transmits the soul (νοῦς) from parent to offspring (*GA* II, 736ᵃ 24 ff.).[22] This account is generalized by the Stoics to provide a thoroughly naturalistic account of the transmission of reason (λόγος), not just from one generation to the next, but from person to person, and between the person and the rest of the cosmos. On the Stoic account, a tension in the *pneuma* and its surrounding passive matter constitutes organic systems of increasing complexity. Man is one such system, and like the others he is a mixture of *pneuma* and passive matter. The *pneuma*, which is mixed with blood, circulates through an intricate internal system which has its centre in the directive faculty (ἡγεμονικόν) and terminates in the five senses and the speech and genital organs. There is input into the system through the sense organs and output through the speech organs and genitals, the former emit-

---

[22] See the commentary in D. M. Balme, *Aristotle's De partibus animalium I and De generatione animalium I* (Oxford, 1972), 156–65.

ting external discourse (λόγος) which reflects man's internal reasoning, the latter the 'seeds of reason' (λόγοι σπερματικόι) whereby one animal generates soul in another. The medical writers, with whom the notion of *pneuma* as a vital spirit linking organism and soul originated, also adopt a radically naturalistic perspective. The powers of imagination, reason, and memory were commonly thought to have their site in the cerebral ventricles, for example, and the physicians argued that damage to these could be associated with specific cognitive and psychological disorders.

Naturalism was to undergo a revival in the Renaissance, but the source was neither the Stoics nor even the medical tradition so much as Alexandrian Aristotelianism. Alexander of Aphrodisias' naturalistic interpretation of Aristotle had been dismissed as offering a crude biological reductionism by many medieval and Renaissance writers, but when the actual text of Alexander was made known in the 1480s such a view was no longer easy to sustain. The Alexandrian interpretation of Aristotle was taken up and developed by Pomponazzi in his *De immortalitate animae* of 1516. Pomponazzi argued there that each living human body has an individual soul, that this soul is the material form of the body, that it is generated by the parents and does not arise as a result of a special act of creation (as Aquinas had argued), and finally that it is not capable of existing without the body. Like Alexander, but contrary to the medical tradition, Pomponazzi is careful to argue that knowing does not take place in any localized part of the body, but rather in the body as a whole, since the intellect includes all the powers of the body. This account, he maintains, is consonant with Aristotle and natural reason, but he concedes, principally on theological grounds, that the soul must participate in immortality to some extent, although such an idea cannot be grasped in terms of natural reason.[23]

---

[23] On Pomponazzi's account see C. Trinkaus, *In Our Image and Likeness* (2 vols., London, 1970), vol. ii, ch. XI; also Randall's intro. to the translation of the *De immortalitate* in E. Cassirer, P. O. Kristeller, and J. H. Randall (eds.), *The Renaissance Philosophy of Man* (Chicago, 1948), 257–79. On the contrast between the Alexandrian and Averroist interpretations of Aristotle, see H. Skulsky, 'Paduan Epistemology and the Doctrine of One Mind', *Journal for the History of Philosophy*, 6 (1968), 341–61.

A diametrically opposed position can also be developed on the basis of a reading of Aristotle. Whereas Pomponazzi's naturalism denies the immortality of the soul because of the close association of the soul and the body, the transcendentalist position accepts the immortality of the soul by denying it any close association with the body. Aristotle maintains that part of the soul (ψυχή) does not perish (e.g. *Metaph. Λ*, 1070ᵃ 21–6) and that what cannot perish cannot have been generated (e.g. *Cael.* II, 282ᵃ 31), as well as stating explicitly that reason (νοῦς) is eternal (*de An.* III, 430ᵃ 17). This 'part of the soul' or 'reason' must be independent of particular bodies, which are subject to generation and corruption, and on the transcendentalist interpretation this is taken to imply that it is independent of any matter. Now Aristotle is explicit that whatever is independent of matter and not individuated by it can only be one in number (*Metaph. Λ*, 1075ᵃ 5–10). This is how the Averroist doctrine of 'one mind' comes about. On the Averroist conception—which we find in Averroës and his Arab followers, in Siger of Brabant and others in the thirteenth and fourteenth centuries, and in Nifo in the sixteenth century—the human being is a composite of animal body, which is a mixture of the four elements, and 'cogitative soul'. The cogitative soul is the material form of the body and provides it with powers of sensation and imagination. It comes into being with the body and dies with it. But, it is argued, there must also be a soul which, in true Aristotelian fashion, understands things by taking on, or becoming, their forms. Such a soul cannot be the form of any particular body, Averroës maintained, and it is something which all men partake of in so far as they are engaged in knowing. In the cognitive process this rational soul or intellect combines with the individual person's cogitative soul to form the speculative or theoretical intellect, by which that person thinks and knows. The upshot of this account is that there is a single intellect in mankind, and this enjoys an impersonal immortality.

Despite its clearly Aristotelian origins, Randall has pointed to a strongly Platonic element in this approach, namely the view that a mind that can grasp eternal and unchanging truths must itself be eternal and unchanging, and not bound by the limits of any particular body.[24] This intellect comes to be seen as the intellect of the human species in the development of Averroism in the later Middle Ages and Renaissance, and this is what lies behind the view that, if truth is to be kept alive and accessible, it must be kept alive in individual minds, and that this is what the teacher passes on to the pupil. Here, of course, we have a characteristically humanist theme, and Averroism gradually comes to take on a number of humanist overtones, for instance the view that knowledge is not a fragmentary individual possession but something both essentially collective and transmitted from antiquity.

The Averroist account was subjected to a number of criticisms from the thirteenth century onwards. The most cogent of these originate with Aquinas who, in his *De unitate intellectus, contra Averroistas*,[25] staunchly opposes the idea of the indivisibility of the intellect and its independence from the body. An indivisible intellect, he argues, would have the absurd consequence of making Socrates and Plato the one person, whereas a completely independent intellect is intuitively implausible since it would mean that the soul and the body would be no more intimately connected than oxen and a cart, and there would in effect be two people (one corresponding to the cogitative soul and the other to the rational soul or intellect) in every individual.

Whereas the Alexandrian naturalists had integrated the soul or intellect and the body, they had done so at the price of denying (or at least failing to account for) the immortality of the soul. And whereas the Averroist transcendentalists had guaranteed the immortality of the soul, this was at the price of denying personal immortality. Aquinas wanted to secure the Christian doctrine of personal immortality, and this required him to give a new account of the relation between the intellect and the cognitive powers of the corporeal faculties. His solution is to argue that the material on

---

[24] Cf. Randall, intro. to *De immortalitate*, in Cassirer, Kristeller, and Randall, *Renaissance Philosophy of Man*, pp. 262 ff., to which my account in this paragraph is indebted.

[25] See Thomas Aquinas, *On the Unity of the Intellect Against the Averroists*, ed. and trans. B. H. Zedler (Milwaukee, 1968). The editor's intro. provides a good summary of the issues.

which the intellect works must derive from our corporeal faculties: the body, via the senses, provides the *phantasiai* which are the basis of all knowledge. But Aquinas draws a sharp distinction between the kinds of cognitive grasp afforded us by the intellect or understanding (*intellectus*), and the reasoning (*ratio*) which is the cognitive activity of our corporeal faculties. The *intellectus*/*ratio* dichotomy is a complex one in Aquinas, but the general thrust of the distinction is to mark out a form of direct intuitive grasp of truth from a limited, piecemeal, and often unreliable form of cognitive activity, which is the only route we have to understanding, but which is far from being an infallible route to such understanding. Moreover, and this is an even more important point, when it does lead to understanding, *ratio* annihilates itself: it has served its purpose and disappears in favour of true knowledge, which is conceived on an intuitive basis.[26] So the central contrast is between direct intuition on the one hand, and the ratiocinative processes of imagining, remembering, and inferring on the other.

On the face of it, the notion of *intellectus* here seems somewhat like Aristotle's νοῦς, which is also a cognitive grasp somehow qualitatively different from the actual procedure which enables us to come by that grasp. But there is a crucial difference. For Aristotle, the knowledge which constitutes νοῦς, is not independent of the procedure that yields it. In the case of explicitly syllogistic knowledge, for example, there may be many syllogisms which yield a proposition, and many that yield it in a formally valid way, but only one will yield it in such a way that the attribute is shown to inhere in the subject universally and necessarily, and unless we can construct that syllogism we will not have true understanding. There can be little doubt that Aquinas wishes to adopt an Aristotelian solution to the problem, but the constraints he is operating under render this impossible. These constraints are, on the one hand, the belief in the existence of pure spirits— God and the angels—who know and understand, but who have no

---

[26] The standard account of this question remains J. Peghaire, *Intellectus et ratio selon S. Thomas d'Aquin* (Paris and Ottawa, 1936).

corporeal faculties. On the other hand, the medical tradition from Galen onwards had shown that damage to the brain and nervous system affected the workings of reason, so it was known that our reasoning was in some way connected with the functioning of the cerebral organs. One could yield to one or the other of these constraints, either by maintaining that knowledge and reason were purely functions of the cerebral organs, so that knowledge for us and knowledge for God, who knows without recourse to a corporeal organ, would be quite different; or one could separate our intellect and our corporeal organs as much as possible, holding, on neo-Platonist grounds for example, that true understanding transcended anything we could achieve merely on the basis of the exercise of corporeal faculties. The first of these is clearly heir to the tradition of the *via negativa*, and the second to the tradition of *via affirmativa*. Aquinas offers a third option, still within the tradition of the latter, but which attempts to capture the idea that while we cannot attain to knowledge without the use of our corporeal faculties the successful exercise of those faculties yields something which is not wholly different from the understanding available to pure spirit, and the connection between the two is captured not in terms of identity but in terms of analogy.

I shall return to this aspect of Aquinas's account below. For the moment what I want to stress is that all responses to the question, except Alexandrian naturalism, locate the cognitive processes in a corporeal organ, and understand the exercise of cognition in terms of the functioning of that organ. This view had considerable precedents in antiquity: going beyond Galen, Poseidonius of Byzantium, as a result of research into brain injuries, had not only associated reasoning with corporeal organs but had actually located reason inside the middle ventricle, and Nemesius, an influential Christian Platonist working at the beginning of the fifth century, had placed perception in the anterior ventricles, reason in the middle, and memory in the posterior ventricle. Even Augustine had accepted a ventricular account, suggesting that the posterior ventricle was the seat of motion, while memory resided in the middle ventricle.[27] Neither Thomists nor Averroists seem to have had any doubts about the ventricular theory, and only the Alexandrian naturalists, who (unlike some of the medical writers) were aware of the danger of biological reductionism if they tried to provide the intellect with a specific location, denied the theory. The vast majority of thinkers, who separated the intellect from basic reasoning and cognitive processes, had no qualms about offering a ventricular theory of the latter.

This had an important impact on how inferential reasoning was construed. It leads to such reasoning being explicitly conceived in terms of the exercise of a corporeal faculty, a conception that ties logic and inference closely to one's understanding of a psychological process. Nowhere is this more evident than in the logic textbooks of late scholasticism.[28] The most authoritative textbooks in the late scholastic tradition were those of Franciscus Toletus (*Introductio in dialecticam Aristotelis*, 1561) and Petrus Fonseca (*Institutionum dialecticarum libri octo*, 1564), both of which were reprinted many times up until the mid-seventeenth century. They were standard texts in Jesuit schools and the former was almost certainly amongst the textbooks from which Descartes learned his logic at La Flèche.[29] More sophisticated than the Ramist textbooks and less concerned with reducing logic to pedagogic devices, they offered a version of Aristotelian/Thomist logic which construed its subject matter as a practical enterprise based on Aristotelian/Thomist psychology. Logic on this conception is an explicitly

---

[27] Good summaries of these developments are provided in W. Pagel, 'Medieval and Renaissance Contributions to the Knowledge of the Brain and its Functions', in F. N. L. Poynter (ed.), *The History and Philosophy of Knowledge of the Brain and its Functions* (Oxford, 1958), 95–114, and in E. R. Harvey, *The Inward Wits* (London, 1975). For more detailed accounts see J. Pigeaud, *La Maladie de l'âme* (Paris, 1981), and G. Verbeke, *L'Évolution de la doctrine de pneuma du Stoïcisme à S. Augustin* (Paris and Louvain, 1945).

[28] Cf. W. Risse, *Die Logik der Neuzeit*; and esp. his 'Zur Vorgeshichte der cartesischen Methodenlehre', *Archiv für Geschichte der Philosophie*, 45 (1963), 269–91. My summary in the following paragraph is based largely on pp. 284–9 of this paper. See also ch. 1 of E. J. Ashworth, *Language and Logic in the Post-Medieval Period* (Dordrecht, 1974). On the texts, W. Risse, *Bibliographia logica: Verzeichnis der Druckschriften zur Logik mit Angabe ihre Fundorte*, i: *1472–1800* (Hildesheim, 1965) is invaluable.

[29] See E. Gilson's discussion of the authors whom Descartes would have studied at La Flèche, in his *La Liberté chez Descartes et la théologie* (Paris, 1913), 5–33.

normative theory of thought, a theory of the regulation of the functions of cognition. Toletus and Fonseca were not the only commentators to treat logic in these terms, but they were easily the most influential, and through the efforts of Fonseca's followers at Coimbra, who developed a full-scale treatment of logic as a practical theory concerned with guiding acts of the understanding, the approach had become one with a wide circulation by the end of the sixteenth century. A few examples will suffice to give the flavour of this development. Suarez (*Disputationes metaphysicae*, 1597) distinguishes metaphysics, which deals with being as such, and logic, which directs acts of the understanding, and is therefore concerned with the process of knowing and not with what is known. Josephus Blanch (*Commentarii in universam Aristotelis logicam*, 1612) considers this process as a real psychological thought process, and Antonius Casilius (*Introductio in Aristotelis logicam*, 1629) presents it as an *actio vitalis*, thereby effectively tying logic to medical theory. Chrysostomus Cabero (*Brevis summularum recapitulatio*, 1623) poses the question of inference in terms of whether logic exercises a natural constraint or norm which is morally binding on thought. Finally, Raphael Aversa (*Logica*, 1623) takes a step which is latent in this whole development and, construing logic in a way suggestive of medical conceptions of the healthy functioning of the body, maintains that logic is that ability which remedies the natural weaknesses of reasoning by establishing rules for coming by knowledge.

Here we have, in general terms, the immediate context in which Descartes's conception of inference must be placed. This context is not that of ancient syllogistic, or medieval logic, which had come to an end by the 1530s at the very latest,[30] but rather one shaped by Ramism and late scholastic psychologism.

---

[30] Cf. E. J. Ashworth, 'The Eclipse of Medieval Logic', in N. Kretzman, A. Kenny, and J. Pinborg (eds.), *The Cambridge History of Later Medieval Philosophy* (Cambridge, 1982), 787–96.

THE NATURAL LIGHT OF REASON

The framework for Descartes's conception of inference, shaped as it is by Ramism and late scholasticism, has a number of significant features. On the one hand, there are two conceptions which the Ramists and the late scholastics held in common. They conceive of inference as an aid to knowledge, that is, it is not constitutive of knowledge in any sense. Secondly, inference is conceived as a function of corporeal faculties, on a par with memory and imagination. On the other hand, there are specific claims that distinguish the two schools. The Ramists maintained that rules of inference were to be replaced by or reduced to classificatory techniques. The late scholastics argued that inference is a psychological process to be distinguished from understanding, which is dependent upon that psychological process but is something over and above it. Bearing in mind this quite specific context, Descartes's own views can be summarized in three points. First, scientific knowledge is arrived at by 'intuition' and 'deduction', and there is no need for syllogistic or rules of inference. Second, these operations require no explication since they are simple and primitive. Third, the pure light of reason is in any case only obscured by attempting to supplement it in any way. Let us look at these in turn.

Descartes claims that his method explains how scientific knowledge is arrived at by 'intuition' and 'deduction'. This method was as much as anything else an alternative to Ramism, although the opposition was not made explicit by Descartes: it was left to Arnauld's *Port-Royal Logic* to do this.[31] Ramus, as we have seen, construed method in pedagogic terms and, having defined dialectic in the traditional way as 'the art of disputing well', divorced the method regulating dialectic from empirical considerations, tying it instead to classification and memory. Descartes, on the other hand, wants method to serve as a logic of discovery, and he wants it to be empirical. Ramus' method refers all questions back to an already

---

[31] On this whole question see Howell, *Logic and Rhetoric in England*.

existing storehouse of knowledge, whereas Descartes is reluctant to accord the contents of this storehouse the title of knowledge at all. Descartes's concern, then, is to develop a method which will enable us to come by new and genuine knowledge. This method is not unlike the Aristotelian topics in one respect, in that it purports to provide us with a procedure for formulating questions relevant to the enquiry at hand. Moreover, Descartes is not as hostile to experimentation and induction as his more programmatic state-ments might suggest, and these can be incorporated into the method. Descartes's conception of method is, however, far too abstract to provide us with any secure guidance at this level. All that it tells us is that the route to be followed is that of 'intuition' and 'deduction'. As regards the latter, it might appear that Descartes is inconsistent in maintaining on the one hand that deduction is part of the process of attaining scientific knowledge, and on the other that we require no rules of inference. But Descartes does think of deduction as being something that re-quires no regulation. In Rule 2 of the *Regulae* we are told that mistakes in reasoning are never due to faulty inference, the implication being that the latter is just not possible, and in the *Replies to the Second Set of Objections to the Meditations* it is maintained that 'the proper deduction of consequences . . . may be performed by anyone, even the inattentive, provided they remem-ber what has gone before'. (AT vii. 157.) Descartes uses the Latin terms *deducere* and *demonstrare* and their French equivalents *déduire* and *démontrer* with abandon, and they may mean explana-tion, proof, induction, or justification, depending on the context.[32] The shared core of meaning here is no more specific than the comparison of one item with another, or the relating of one item to another. That this is indeed the intended core of Descartes's conception is made clear in Rule 14 of the *Regulae*:

In every train of reasoning it is merely by comparison that we attain to a precise knowledge of the truth. Here is an example: all *A* is *B*, all *B* is *C*,

---

[32] For details see D. M. Clarke, *Descartes' Philosophy of Science* (Manchester, 1982), 63–74 and 207–10.

therefore all *A* is *C*. Here we compare with one another what we are searching for and what we are given, viz. *A* and *C*, in respect of the fact that each is *B*, and so on. But, as we have pointed out on a number of occasions, because the forms of the syllogism are of no aid in perceiving the truth about things, it will be better for the reader to reject them altogether and to conceive that all knowledge whatsoever, other than that which consists in the simple and pure intuition of single independent objects, is a matter of the comparison of two things or more with each other. In fact practically the whole task set the human reason consists in preparing for this operation; for when it is open and simple, we need no aid from art, but are bound to rely upon the light of nature alone, in beholding the truth which comparison gives us. (AT x. 439–40.)

The difference between intuition and deduction lies in the fact that whereas the latter consists in grasping the relations between a number of propositions, intuition (*intuitus*) consists in grasping one proposition or in grasping a necessary connection between two propositions, and it is equated with clear and distinct perception. As Descartes describes it in Rule 3 of the *Regulae*:

By *intuitus* I understand not fluctuating reliance on the senses, nor the misleading judgement of an imagination which puts things together in the wrong way, but the apprehension which the mind, pure and attentive, gives us so easily and so distinctly that we are thereby freed from all doubt as to what it is that we are apprehending. (AT x. 368.)[33]

In the limiting case, as we have seen, deduction reduces to intuition: we run through the deduction so quickly that we no longer have to rely on memory, with the result that we 'have the whole in intuition' before us at a single time. So in the limiting case, knowledge consists not in intuition and deduction as such, but simply in intuition.

Notice, however, that as well as consisting in a grasp of a necessary connection between two limiting terms, which is what deduction reduces to, intuition can also consist in a grasp of a single proposition. On the face of it, it might seem that the first alone is relevant to Descartes's conception of inference. But the

[33] See D. M. Clarke, *Descartes' Philosophy of Science* (Manchester, 1982), pp. 58–63 for an invaluable discussion of *intuitus*.

second is if anything even more revealing for, given the way in which Descartes presents the distinction between intuition and deduction, the obvious model is a geometrical one, in which we grasp certain axioms, and so on, and deduce from these geometrical theorems. One problem with axiomatic systems—whether in geometry, logic, or any other formalized domain—is that one might be misled into thinking that axioms are indispensable, serving a special role for which rules of inference alone would be inappropriate. Since Gentzen, we know this to be false, and the various forms of 'natural deduction' and other axiomless systems have distinct advantages over axiomatic systems.[34] Descartes saw matters very differently. It is not just a case of axioms being necessary; Descartes clearly thinks that for something to be an axiom it must have special intrinsic properties, such as self-evidence and indubitability, which enable it to play the role it does. Propositions meeting these requirements are grasped by intuition, not deduction, and form the basis for any subsequent deduction. Although *intuitus* disappears from Descartes's vocabulary in his later writings, this general conception does not, and indeed its crowning achievement is the *cogito*. The *cogito* is effectively an intuition of a basic premiss which, because of its indubitability and self-evidence, can be grasped independently of anything else, including rules of inference. It forms the starting-point for knowledge and the paradigm for knowledge in that, while it is a grasp of a single proposition, to get to other propositions one grasps necessary connections between this and the others, remembering that, in the limiting case, this grasp should itself take the form of an intuition.

In construing deduction in terms of intuition rather than rules of inference, one thing that Descartes is doing is ruling out any attempt at analysing inferential steps: in the limiting case, there are no such steps. Inference cannot be analysed on Descartes's view because it is simple and primitive. He gives us no details of what

[34] See W. Kneale, 'The Province of Logic', in H. D. Lewis (ed.), *Contemporary British Philosophy*, *Third Series* (London, 1956), 235–62, and I. Hacking, 'What is Logic?', *Journal of Philosophy*, 76 (1979), 285–319.

he has in mind here, but he makes the same kind of claim about truth in a letter to Mersenne of 16 October 1639, and here he does spell out what he means. Discussing Herbert of Cherbury's *De veritate*, which replies to scepticism by providing a general account of truth, on the grounds that if we understand what truth is we will be able to show that scepticism rests upon a misunderstanding of truth, Descartes writes:

In general [the author] takes a very different path in this book from the one I have followed. He examines what truth is; I have never had any doubts about this, because it seems a notion so transcendentally clear that nobody can be ignorant of it. There are many ways of examining a balance before using it, but there is no way to learn what truth is, if one does not know its nature. For what reason could we have for accepting anything which could teach us the nature of truth if we did not know that it was true, that is to say, if we did not know truth? Of course it is possible to tell the meaning of the word to someone who did not know the language, and tell him that the word *truth*, in its strict sense, denotes the conformity of thought with its object, and that when it is attributed to things outside thought, it means only that they can be the objects of true thoughts, whether in our minds or in God's. But we can give no definition of logic which will help anyone to discover its nature. And I believe the same holds of many other things which are very simple and known naturally, such as shape, size, movement, place, time and so on. For if you try to define these things you only obscure them and cause confusion . . . The author takes universal consent as the criterion of his truths; whereas I have no criterion for mine except the light of nature. (AT ii. 596–7.)

That is to say, while we can define truth, such a definition could not be explanatory, for nothing can be clearer than truth: we can explain what the word means in the sense of explaining that this is the word that we use of a certain phenomenon, but not in the sense of giving an account of that phenomenon in other terms which are better understood. The argument requires careful wording however. Descartes is not making the specious claim that if the *analysans* is to capture all and only what is meant by the *analysandum* then the *analysandum* must tell us the same thing as the *analysans*, in which case we have learned nothing. Rather, the reasoning behind the claim is that unless we had a prior under-standing of truth, we could not understand a definition of it, for we would have to be able to grasp that the definition itself was true if we were to understand it. Unless we had already grasped the difference between truth and falsity, it would be wholly obscure what role definitions could play. If one takes Descartes's own example, the conformity of a thought with its object, whether one construes that object as being an intentional object or whether, as with the correspondence theory of truth, one takes it as a real object (or state of affairs), then Descartes is surely right. To say that truth consists in such a relation is to say that it is true that it consists in that relation. This is not the way to enlightenment about what truth consists in.

Nevertheless, to say that truth is primitive and simple is not to say that we have a primitive and simple way of determining, for any sentence, whether it is true. This is where the problem in the closely related case of inference arises. The parallel between inference and truth is not one of analogy. If it were, then Descartes could simply deny that one can define inference in terms which are better understood. But he does not do this. Quite the contrary, he effectively provides just such a definition in maintaining that, in the limiting case, inference comes down to the intuitive grasp of a necessary connection between premiss and conclusion. What Descartes denies is that this grasp can be justified, on the grounds that anything which would justify it would have to presuppose it. It is here that we have the parallel with truth, and in fact it turns out to be more than merely a parallel, for our intuitive and instantaneous grasp of inferential connection is an intuitive and instantaneous grasp of a truth. But how do we know that what we grasp is in fact a truth? To say that the 'light of nature' or 'light of reason' must be our guide is unhelpful without some specification of how this 'light' works. Does it enable us to recognize some intrinsic quality possessed only by truths, or perhaps to partition propositions on the basis of some other criterion?

The extent to which Descartes's account here is psychologistic is open to question. He is certainly not maintaining that logical relations are to be construed ultimately as psychological relations, as the late scholastics occasionally did. He is completely opposed to that kind of psychologism. The whole thrust of his argument is to deny that truth and inference can be explained in reductive terms, whether psychological, medical, physiological, or whatever. But there is still a grey area. Consider his remark in a letter to Regius (24 May 1640) that 'our mind is of such a nature that it cannot help assenting to what it conceives clearly' (AT iii. 64). What our mind conceives clearly and distinctly is what it conceives by the light of nature or the light of reason. There can be no doubt that one thing that is being claimed here is that, when the mind conceives something clearly and distinctly, it has compelling and incontrovertible evidence for the truth of what it conceives. But what is he claiming over and above this? He is certainly not maintaining that my conceiving something clearly and distinctly makes it true. What I conceive must already be true, in that we cannot grasp truth in terms other than clarity and distinctness. Clarity and distinctness are constitutive, for us, of what truth consists in. This makes Descartes's account of truth epistemic, but it does not make it psychologistic. The suggestion of psychologism in Descartes's account comes from the fact that when we grasp something clearly and distinctly, it is our grasp that is clear and distinct, not what is grasped. 'I can establish as a general rule', he tells us in *Meditation III*, 'that all things which I perceive very clearly and distinctly are true' (AT vii. 35). In other words, the grasp of a truth is manifested in some sort of psychological clarity experienced by the knowing subject. The question is whether one wants to call this 'psychologism': it is not psychologism in the sense in which many eighteenth- and especially nineteenth-century writers on logic and mathematics were psychologistic. But whatever one calls it, it is a difficult and problematic conception.

The problems come to the fore when we consider another aspect of Descartes's account. As I have indicated, Descartes rejects any attempt to elucidate truth, holding it to be primitive and incapable of further elucidation. This approach rules out any attempt to provide a reductive account of truth, such as that offered by psychologism, but it also rules out any non-reductive attempt to elucidate the nature of truth. This is going too far. There are many questions that we can ask about truth with a view to elucidation which do not involve our falling into circularity or reductionism at all. We can ask whether there are any expressions extensionally equivalent to '. . . is true' and what these have in common with that expression, we can ask what truth consists in, or what it is that distinguishes true sentences from false sentences, or what we recognize as tests for truth, or what the connection between truth ánd other semantic notions is, or whether something can be neither true nor false, and so on. Truth must be taken as primitive in some contexts, but not in all, and this much can surely be accepted with accepting reductionism. Descartes's account blocks off further elucidation because it establishes the primitiveness of truth in too strong a way. Consequently, when we are asked to justify something fundamental, such as an inferential principle, we are forced back ultimately on to a form of psychological clarity experienced by the knowing subject.

The point can be brought out in a rather striking way by comparing Descartes and Aristotle. It is interesting to note just how wide the gulf is between Descartes's solution to the problem and the paradigmatic discursive justification of an inferential principle: Aristotle's justification of the law of non-contradiction. In *Metaphysics* Γ4, Aristotle points out that proofs must come to an end somewhere, otherwise we could be involved in an infinite regress. Hence there must be something that we can rely upon without proof, and he takes as his example the law of non-contradiction.[35] The law is justified by showing that an opponent who denies it must, in denying it, actually assume its truth, and by showing that arguments which apparently tell against it—for example the Protagorean relativist arguments which deduce from the fact that a thing may seem sweet to one person and bitter to another that it is both sweet and bitter (i.e. both sweet and not

---

[35] See the discussion in ch. 6 of J. Lear, *Aristotle and Logical Theory* (Cambridge, 1980).

sweet)—cannot be sustained. It is here that the discursive conception of inference shows its mettle, and Descartes can offer nothing analogous. It is something ambiguously psychological—the 'light of reason' or the 'light of nature'—that stops the regress in Descartes's conception.

There is another aspect of Descartes's argument, however. In rejecting the idea that inference is to be guided by rules, what he is concerned with is the rules of reasoning offered by Ramus' method and the Jesuit 'directions for thinking' (*directio ingenii*). His argument is that we cannot be taught what an inference is: we cannot be taught to reason. Descartes, of course, offers his own 'rules for the direction of the mind' and 'discourse on the method of rightly conducting reason', but these presuppose not only that one can reason but that one never in fact makes mistakes of inference, as we have seen, and hence tend to be negative, often consisting of little more than trivial hints about how to avoid various errors due to inattentiveness, unnecessary complexity, and so on. Unlike the Ramist and Jesuit theories, they are not designed to instruct one how to think. This is evident, for example, from his remarks in the *Search after Truth by the Light of Nature*, written in the 1640s:

I cannot prevent myself from stopping you here, ... [to] make you consider what common sense can do if it is well directed. In fact, is there anything in what you have said which is not exact, which is not legitimately argued and deduced? And yet all the consequences are drawn without logic or a formula for the argument, thanks to the simple light of reason and good sense which is less subject to error when it acts alone and by itself than when it anxiously tries to follow a thousand diverse rules which human art and idleness have discovered, less to perfect it than to corrupt it. (AT x. 521.)[36]

In rejecting 'rules of inference' Descartes is not concerned with logical laws as such, but with rules which purport to teach one how to think properly. The broad way in which dialectic had been

---

[36] Cf. also Descartes to Mersenne, 27 Feb. 1637 (AT i. 349), where Descartes insists that the aim of the *Discourse on Method* is not to teach method but to describe it.

conceived in the Renaissance led to a conflation of these two. In the 'Conversation with Burman', Descartes says that his criticisms of logic (in the *Discourse on Method*) are really criticisms of dialectic, rather than criticisms of logic proper:

This really applies to Dialectic, which teaches us how to hold forth on all subjects, rather than to Logic, which provides demonstrative proofs on all subjects. In this way it undermines good sense, rather than building on it. For in diverting our attention and making us digress into the stock arguments and headings, which are irrelevant to the thing under discussion, it diverts us from the actual nature of the thing itself. (AT v. 175.)

While this explicit distinction is an afterthought on Descartes's part, the implicit distinction is there in the earlier writings. It is an important distinction, and if we adhere to it we can separate out with greater precision the issues to which Descartes's criticisms are directed.

We can distinguish between the question of the justification of basic logical principles and the justification of particular inferences, and we can break this last question down into two further ones: what inferences do we count as canonical, and what is the relation of other inferences to these? In putting the question in this way, a direct comparison with Aristotle is possible. In the *Prior Analytics*, Aristotle classified syllogisms into three figures, and the following can serve as examples of the general forms:

Barbara (Figure 1)	*Cesare* (Figure 2)	*Darapti* (Figure 3)
A holds of all B	N holds of no Ξ	Σ holds of all P
B holds of all Γ	N holds of all M	Π holds of all P
A holds of all Γ	Ξ holds of no M	Σ holds of some Π

Aristotle maintains that first-figure syllogisms are perfect or complete ($\tau \acute{\epsilon} \lambda \epsilon \iota o s$), whereas those of the second and third figures are not, and he provides techniques for converting the latter into the former. Second- and third-figure syllogisms can be formally valid, yet Aristotle is not completely satisfied unless they can be converted into a canonical first-figure form. The reason for this, as

Patzig has argued in detail, is that there is an obvious transitivity of connections in the first-figure syllogism which is lacking in the others.[37] We can, as it were, see at a glance that the syllogism is valid. Is this very different from Descartes's procedure? Descartes tells us that in the case of lengthy inferences we must go through the inferential steps more and more quickly so that in the end we grasp the premisses and conclusion in one instantaneous step. In doing this we assimilate inference to the canonical case of *intuitus*. There are differences, of course. Descartes is not concerned with inferences which are problematic for reasons other than their length, whereas for Aristotle the number of steps in an inference is not a logical problem. A much more important difference, however, lies in the criteria by which canonical forms are singled out. Aristotle's aim is to find an argument-form which proves irresistible to an opponent, and this parallels his account of the justification of basic principles, which as we have seen is conceived on similarly discursive lines. Descartes's criterion is provided in both cases by some form of psychological clarity experienced by the knowing subject. But there is some common ground of problems between Aristotle and Descartes, despite the fact that these problems are posed in a discursive context in the one case and in a 'psychological' one in the other. This 'psychological context' requires further classification before we can assess it fully, but two points can be made which may go some way to dispelling the idea that the resort to posing questions of inference in such a context is totally damning.

First, there is the question of the respective merits of the facultative and discursive models where questions of the logic of discovery are concerned. Questions of discovery are intimately tied to general questions of inference in the seventeenth century, and Aristotelian syllogistic was rejected largely because it was expected to, and failed to, provide a logic of discovery. This expectation was mistaken—if the seventeenth-century natural philosophers were

---

[37] Cf. G. Patzig, *Die aristotelische Syllogistik* (Göttingen, 1963), *passim*. I have ignored many details, such as the fact that some non-categorical first-figure syllogisms are not 'perfect', because these have no bearing on our present concerns.

looking for a method of discovery in Aristotle they should have turned their attention not to syllogistic but to the topics—but mistaken or not it spelled the end of syllogistic. Now in the context of deductive inference, the choice is basically that between convincing oneself, on the facultative model, and convincing others, on the discursive model. There is no clear advantage for one side or the other here. But in the context of discovery, there is an immense advantage for the facultative conception. The discursive conception requires common ground between oneself and one's opponents, and in seventeenth-century natural philosophy that would not have been at all forthcoming. In other words, the case against conceiving of inference in a discursive way links up strongly with the case against appealing in one's enquiries to what is generally accepted rather than to what is the case. It is, of course, from this that the immense polemical strength of Descartes's attack on syllogistic derives.

Second, Descartes managed to pose questions central to the nature of inference which are literally inconceivable in Ramist thought, with its inability to give any account of relations between propositions not germane to pedagogical classification, and in late scholastic thought, where a psychological reduction robs inference of any specifically logical features. Of central importance here is the issue of logic, and inference generally, as an 'aid to knowledge'. Both the Ramists and the late scholastics, as I have indicated, are committed to a conception of logic/dialectic as an aid to knowledge, that is, as something not constitutive of knowledge in its own right. By making inference in the limiting case a form of intuition, which for him is knowledge *par excellence*, Descartes takes the ground from under this conception. The result is that he can raise questions of inference in a rudimentary but recognizably logico-philosophical context. The difference between Descartes and his contemporaries is that, for Descartes, inference is not something that our corporeal organs engage in so that the information provided thereby can be passed on to the incorporeal intellect, which unfortunately cannot get its information in any other way. Rather, this is what our intellect, when it is acting through an *intuitus*, *tells* us is knowledge. Descartes is able to effect this radical rethinking of inference because of his doctrine of eternal truths, to which we now turn.

ETERNAL TRUTHS: A HUMAN MODEL FOR COGNITION

At a first glance, the doctrine of eternal truths appears to threaten, rather than complement, the doctrine of intuition. It commits one to the view, for example, that there is, at least at one level, no real distinction to be made between necessary and contingent truths for, even though Descartes is not claiming that we could actually conceive of a world in which necessary truths are false, the fact is that no truths are necessary as far as God is concerned, and the effective upshot of this is that, for God, all truths are contingent. And since, after all, it is God who provides us with our truths in the first place on Descartes's view, this is somewhat disconcerting. Moreover, if God is free to change all truths at will, then even those truths which we grasp in an *intuitus* are called into question. On the face of it, the doctrine of eternal truths has the potential to bring down Descartes's whole conception of knowledge, and *a fortiori* of inference. If we are to throw light on the bearing of this doctrine on the issue of inference, there are two questions that we must answer. First, what motivates Descartes to adopt a doctrine so counterintuitive that not one of his predecessors, contemporaries, or successors was even tempted by it? Secondly, to what extent is our grasp of truths, whether inferential or not, affected by the fact that the cognitive faculties that enable us to exercise that grasp do not allow us to comprehend those truths in a way which could register any understanding of their creator's comprehension of them?

Marion has recently shown in detail that Descartes's doctrine of eternal truths is a reaction to two currents of thought about the relation between our knowledge and God's knowledge.[38] The

---

[38] J.-L. Marion, *Sur la théologie blanche de Descartes* (Paris, 1981). The two currents are discussed on pp. 27–159 and pp. 161–227 respectively.

principal figure in the first current, which is that of scholastic philosophy, is Suarez, and the evidence indicates that much of Descartes's account is specifically directed against Suarez.[39] Suarez's account is a revision of Aquinas's doctrine. Aquinas had developed the standard scholastic compromise on the question of whether attribution of properties to God and creation was univocal or equivocal. Starting from a theologically motivated assumption of equivocality, he develops an account in which this equivocality is bridged by conceiving of the relation between creation and God analogically. Underlying this analogical conception is the doctrine of exemplarism, according to which divine ideas are exemplars or patterns, on the models of which God created the world, but such exemplars are imperfectly exemplified in creation. Marion shows how the ontological basis of exemplarism subsequently comes to be replaced by an epistemological emphasis, so that eternal truths, for example, are no longer construed as exemplars proper, patterns on which creation is modelled, but rather as objects to be known by both God and us. In this way exemplarism becomes transformed into the problem of whether our ideas can represent these eternal truths, and in this changed context a new problem comes to the fore, which undermines the basis for the Thomist doctrine of analogy. It is Duns Scotus who points out that, in so far as we are concerned in metaphysics with the question of being-*qua*-being, analogy is not enough: we must have a single unitary conception of being that is logically prior to the distinctions between (and any analogies between) created and uncreated being, and finite and infinite being. Suarez, on the basis of this type of argument, takes univocity as his starting-point and deploys analogy in a restricted range. In particular, he is happy to allow that there are general constraints on representing objects to any intellect, whether human or divine. While a full comparison with Aquinas is not possible here, because of the shift of context from an ontological concern with exemplarism to an epistemological concern with representation, there is one central overwhelming difference

---

[39] See ibid. pp. 27–8.

between Aquinas and Suarez which, for our limited purposes, can be abstracted from context, and this is that whereas Aquinas conceives of our knowledge of eternal truths and God's knowledge of these truths on the basis of analogy, Suarez conceives of them on the basis of univocity. And Descartes conceives of them on the basis of equivocality. In fact his doctrine is advocated as a response to the problematic and unstable nature of Suarez's compromise. Although eternal truths are understood univocally and hence are the same for God as they are for us, Suarez tells us explicitly that we can have no insight into how God knows them to be true. This is what Descartes specifically objects to. Here his position is indeed the exact contrary of Leibniz, in the sense that Descartes and Leibniz can be seen as taking up different horns of Suarez's dilemma. Descartes's understanding of eternal truths as equivocal turns on his accepting that we cannot have any insight into how God knows them to be true, so we cannot then say that such truths are the same for God as they are for us. Leibniz's position can be understood as the exact opposite of this, as an advocation of univocity on the basis that he takes as given that eternal truths must be the same for us and for God, and hence we must have some insight into how God knows them to be true: and we do have such insight, in that we can say that God knows them to be true because he knows their proofs. The second current of thought that Descartes is reacting against is really the precursor of this Leibnizian view. This second current is the nascent tradition of mathematical physics, and Kepler, Mersenne, and Galileo all take the view that our grasp of mathematical truths is no different from that of God.

It would take us too far from our topic to attempt to follow through the theological, metaphysical, and other considerations underlying all these different accounts. The crucial point is that the context in which Descartes's account is formulated is in the first instance not mathematical or logical but theological: it is a response to a clearly unstable conception of eternal truths, a conception which pulls us in two opposing directions, complete univocity and complete equivocality.[40]

[40] Marion (ibid. pp. 455–6), perhaps inspired by Gilson in this respect, argues that the

There is an epistemological side to the question, however, which turns on Descartes's conception of what truth consists in and how we recognize it. Descartes maintains, in the letter to Regius cited above, that 'our mind is of such a nature that it cannot refuse to assent to what it conceives clearly'. What the mind cannot refuse to assent to here is the truth of what it so conceives. Consequently, Descartes's claim is:

A: If p is conceived by me clearly and distinctly, I cannot refuse to assent to the truth of p.

Now if I cannot refuse to assent to the truth of p, this is presumably because I am justified in assenting to the truth of p, and surely I am only justified in assenting to the truth of p in the case where p is true. Fleshing A out in this way we arrive at:

B: If p is conceived by me clearly and distinctly, p is true.

In the *Reply to the Second Set of Objections*, however, Descartes makes a claim that appears to be a direct contradiction of B. He writes:

For what difference would it make to us if someone pretended that this truth, of which we are so strongly persuaded, appears false to God or to the angels, and hence is, in absolute terms, false? Why should we concern ourselves with this absolute falsity, when we neither believe it nor have the least suspicion of it? For we are supposing a belief or conviction so strong that nothing can remove it, and this conviction is in every respect the same as absolute certainty. (AT vii. 145/ix$_1$. 113–14.)

In short, I might be certain of p notwithstanding the absolute falsity of p. If we equate certainty with the having of clear and distinct ideas, then there is clearly a discrepancy between this absolute falsity claim and B.

---

original Thomist solution, which depends on the doctrine of analogy, is the path that Descartes should have taken. I find this baffling since so much of his account shows how the shift from an exemplarist to a representational context robs analogy of its original value and motivation. To keep the analogy we would have to return to exemplarism, and it is difficult to imagine what grounds anyone could have for suggesting that this would be a move in the right direction, although Hobbes, Locke, Malebranche, and Vico all at times hold something akin to exemplarism: see my 'Vico and the Maker's Knowledge Principle', *History of Philosophy Quarterly*, 3 (1986), 29–44.

One way in which the discrepancy can be overcome is to say that Descartes's claim is not B but:

C: If p is conceived by me clearly and distinctly, p is certain.

This is compatible with A, which we know Descartes holds, and also with the absolute falsity claim. But C is ambiguous as it stands. It can mean either of the following:

C':   If p is conceived by me clearly and distinctly, p is something of which I am certain.

C'':   If p is conceived by me clearly and distinctly, p is something of which I am entitled to be certain.

C' says nothing about our grounds for belief, but merely identifies the psychological state I am in when I have a clear and distinct conception. It is compatible with p being false. But there can be no doubt that Descartes means something stronger than this: it is clear that he *is* concerned with our grounds for belief. C'', on the other hand, does concern our grounds for belief, but we must be careful not to make it too strong. One might be tempted, for example, to argue that the only thing that can entitle me to be certain of p is its truth. To be certain of p is, after all, to be certain of the truth of p, and Descartes himself talks of 'this *truth* of which we are so strongly persuaded'. But to say that it can only be the truth of p that entitles me to be certain of p is too strong. For to argue in this way is to make C'', and hence C, equivalent to B. Clearly C'' will only be a successful interpretation if it maintains its epistemic character. We can do this by taking our entitlement to certainty to derive not from truth but from something like maximal evidence. A clear and distinct conception would then derive from the scope and nature of the evidence for p, and if all the relevant evidence pointed to p, and if this evidence were complete, we could say that we are entitled to be certain of the truth of p, even though p may not in fact be true.

But matters are not as straightforward as this, for there are instances in which Descartes is clearly maintaining B. It is of paramount importance here that we distinguish two kinds of certainty: what Descartes calls moral certainty and what (in the Latin edition of the *Principles*) he calls absolute certainty. Moral certainty is described in Principle 205 of Part IV of the *Principles*. It is 'a certainty that suffices for the conduct of our life, though if we regard the absolute power of God, what is morally certain may be uncertain' (AT ix$_2$. 323). As examples of areas in which only moral certainty is possible, he gives his own accounts of magnetism, fire, and matter theory. Two features of moral certainty are worth noting briefly. First, in describing moral certainty here, Descartes makes no mention of our grasping things clearly and distinctly. Rather, he appears to equate moral certainty with something like inference to the best explanation. In the light of this, there must be some question as to how far the doctrine of clarity and distinctness applies to moral certainty, and my discussion of clear and distinct conceptions in what follows in this chapter will be restricted to the context of absolute certainty. Secondly, the only thing that Descartes mentions as potentially undermining moral certainty is the 'absolute power of God'. This is a much stronger form of certainty than that which we would normally associate with 'moral certainty', and it goes beyond anything that would be needed merely for 'the conduct of our life', since it would appear that the only type of doubt that it is subject to is hyperbolic doubt.

These two points are important if we are to understand the contrast between moral and absolute certainty, and why in the case of the latter Descartes appears to maintain *B*. Absolute certainty is unequivocally spelled out in terms of clarity and distinctness, and it is exempted from hyperbolic doubt. It is described in Principle 206 of Part IV of the *Principles* as follows:

The other kind of certainty is that we have when we judge it to be impossible that something should be other than it is. It is based on a very secure metaphysical principle, that, as God is supremely good and the source of all truths, since it is he who has created them, it is certain that the power or faculty that he has given us of distinguishing the true from the false does not mislead us when we use it properly, and so long as it shows us distinctly that a thing is true. This certainty extends to everything that is demonstrated in mathematics; for we see clearly that it is impossible that the sum of two and three should be more or less than five, or that a square have only three sides, etc. (AT ix_2. 324.)

Descartes then goes on to include in this list the existence of the external world, what can be known about this world by the principles of mathematics, and his accounts of the transmission of light and perception.

God's guarantee means that when we are absolutely certain of p, it is the case that we have a clear and distinct conception of p, and that p is true. Our having a clear and distinct conception of p and its being true are connected, but how? It is not our having the clear and distinct conception that makes p true: rather, it is our clear and distinct conception that (in the case of absolute certainty) enables us to grasp the truth of p. What then does make p true? I think there is now general agreement that, for Descartes, it is p's corresponding to reality that makes it true.[41] Problems arise, however, when we ask how God guarantees that what we conceive clearly and distinctly is true. On the face of it, there does not seem to be a great problem. God creates truths, he creates our means of recognizing truths, and he makes sure that the two match one another (at least in the case of absolute certainty). But this kind of approach is not open to Descartes.

To see why, let us begin by imagining a more conventional God than Descartes's. This conventional God is omniscient. He knows, for example, all the truths of mathematics. This is not because he makes them true, however, but because he finds them to be truths. There is an objective realm of things which are true, which God, being omniscient, has complete and immediate access to. We can grasp at least some of these truths, and we can know that what we have grasped are in fact truths in some cases because we have a

---

[41] H. G. Frankfurt, *Demons, Dreamers, and Madmen* (Indianopolis, 1970) attributes a coherence theory of truth to Descartes, but in his 'Descartes on the Consistency of Reason', in M. Hooker (ed.), *Descartes* (Baltimore, 1978), 26–39, he retracts this and opts for the more usual correspondence view. Cf. also C. Larmore, 'Descartes' Psychologistic Theory of Assent', *History of Philosophy Quarterly*, 1 (1984), 61–74.

clear and distinct idea of them, and because God has guaranteed that this clear and distinct idea enables us to identify truths. What we are imagining here is that truth consists in correspondence to reality, that we have an epistemic criterion which, with a divine guarantee, enables us to recognize some truths, and that God presumably has some other (epistemic?) criterion: or perhaps that he does not need such a criterion, he just grasps truths. So far so good. But of course this is not Descartes's God. It is the God of Kepler, Mersenne, and Galileo, who were arguing that, at least in the case of mathematics, we have the same kind of knowledge as God does, only in a reduced degree.[42] God knows all mathematical truths whereas we only know some, but those we do know we know in the same way as, and with the same certainty as, God. Descartes absolutely denies this, as we have seen.

We must therefore revise our picture to take account of Descartes's postulation of equivocality, and his corresponding view that God is not omniscient but cognitively omnipotent: he knows all truths because he creates them. But this is not a change of detail, it alters everything. I have said that, for us, what makes *p* true is its correspondence to reality, and we recognize the truth of *p* by the criterion of clear and distinct ideas. But the distinction between what makes something true and how we recognize its truth is not as sharp as it may seem. This can be shown if we consider the situation of a cognitively omnipotent God. The problem is that we cannot understand what makes something true for such a God because we cannot understand how he recognizes truth. More precisely, it is not possible for us to understand in what sense what a cognitively omnipotent God has created can be, for him, truths. While *we* can regard what he has created as truths, it is far from clear that he can regard them as such. Our ability to designate something a truth depends upon an understanding, albeit only implicit, of what truth consists in, of what we need a notion of truth for and what we use it for. This understanding depends upon our grasp of how truth is manifested and how we

---

[42] For a full discussion and references for Kepler, Mersenne, and Galileo see J.-L. Marion, *Sur la théologie blanche*, pp. 161–227.

test for it; upon our grasp of the systematic difference between our employment of true sentences and false sentences; upon our grasp of the point of separating out inference patterns which are truth-preserving rather than those that preserve some other property. A cognitively omnipotent God might well be able to divide sentences into those that *we* would regard as true and those that *we* would regard as false, but they might as well be designated 'T' and 'F', or '1' and '0', unless he possessed an independent understanding of truth, an understanding which took the form of a grasp of the point of the exercise. For a God who created truths by fiat, such that something is true if and only if it results from such a fiat, such an independent understanding would be wholly irrelevant, and it is the very irrelevance of such an understanding that shows that it is not *truth*, in the sense in which we understand it, that, as far as the cognitively omnipotent God is concerned, he is creating.

In other words, because we have no epistemic grasp of truth-for-God, that is, no way of relating it to what the point of the exercise is for us, we have no grasp of truth-for-God. It is simply not something we can recognize as *truth*: it is something else, we know not what. This poses an immense problem for the idea that our knowledge could have a divine guarantee, for God would be being asked to guarantee something that would surely make as little sense to him as truth-for-God does to us. The equivocality argument, if carried through to its proper conclusion, not only ultimately undermines the idea of a 'good' God—for there is no reason at all why 'good' should not be subject to the same equivocation as every other term—but also *undermines any intelligible connection between God and us.*

Descartes does not, of course, take equivocality this far, although this is where the argument leads. Nevertheless, what he ends up advocating in fact achieves the same epistemological result. But complete equivocality, and an equivocality bridged by divine guarantee, ultimately results in such a radical distancing of God from anything we can say about our knowledge and reasoning processes that God's knowledge and reasoning processes effectively become irrelevant in any account we might give of ours. This is a revolutionary move, for it means that human knowledge can no longer be modelled in any way on divine knowledge. For Descartes, our knowledge is not knowledge in reduced degree, as those figures at the forefront of the scientific revolution—Kepler, Galileo, and Mersenne—thought, but rather knowledge of a completely different kind from God's, since our route to that knowledge must of necessity be different from God's. Employing this conception, Descartes is able to give an uncompromising answer to the traditional cognitive problem of how to reconcile the belief that our reasoning is in some way a function of our cerebral organs, on the one hand, and a belief that there are pure spirits, such as God and the angels, who reason yet have no corporeal faculties, on the other. His answer is flatly to deny that we can say anything about those creatures who reason without recourse to corporeal faculties. In this he is surely right.

Another consequence of this conception is that it enables Descartes to naturalize cognition and epistemology generally; not to the extent of advocating a materialist theory of mind, as one commentator has argued,[43] but to a very considerable extent none the less.[44] This is made possible by dissociating our knowledge from God's, and Descartes can thereby free himself of the constraint of trying, *per impossibile*, to model human knowledge on a wholly inappropriate divine prototype. This of course leaves the problem of how creatures with our corporeally limited and constrained cognitive faculties can have any confidence that those corporeal faculties actually yield knowledge. Descartes's answer to this problem is given concisely in the *Third Meditation*:

. . . God might have endowed me with a nature such that I may have been deceived even concerning things which seemed to me most manifest. And whenever this view of the sovereign power of a God comes into my thought, I must confess that it is easy for him, if he so wishes, to cause me

[43] H. Caton, *The Origin of Subjectivity* (New Haven, 1973).

[44] For details see C. Larmore, 'Descartes' Empirical Epistemology', and N. L. Maull, 'Cartesian Optics and the Geometrization of Nature', both in S. Gaukroger (ed.), *Descartes* (Sussex, 1980), 6–22, 23–40; also J. W. Yolton, *Perceptual Acquaintance from Descartes to Reid* (Oxford, 1984), ch. 1.

to err even in matters which I believe I have the greatest evidence. But, on the other hand, whenever I direct myself towards the things that I believe I conceive very clearly, I am so persuaded by them that I cannot resist saying this: Whoever deceives me, he can never cause me to be nothing while I think I am something, or, it being true now that I exist, some day cause it to be true that I have never existed, or that two and three makes less than five, for anything else that I see clearly cannot be other than I conceive it. (AT vii. 36/ix[1]. 28.)

We simply do not need God's knowledge as a model, only God's guarantee for our knowledge, and this is not such a high price to pay when we realize that it takes us away from a conception of knowledge which is inappropriate and unrealizable.

Descartes played a critical role in what I have identified as the transition from discursive to facultative conceptions of inference, and he did this by providing an account of how inference can both be constitutive of knowledge and yet a cognitive process in which our corporeal faculties engage. It is by rejecting the notion that inference is an aid to knowledge that he is able to do this, and this rejection depends upon his being able to treat our cognitive faculties as being productive of knowledge in their own right, which in turn is only possible if we do not model them on God's faculties. This last point is secured via the doctrine of eternal truths, which thereby plays a fundamental role in Descartes's conception of inference.

This approach is taken further in Leibniz. His univocal model of reasoning should not be seen as something which simply contradicts Descartes's equivocal model; rather, it builds upon it and goes beyond it in certain crucial respects. In attempting to understand proof in terms of intuition, so that we can move directly from premises to conclusion in the one step, Descartes is raising an issue which Leibniz will deal with much more successfully in his account of algebra as a system in which 'we cannot err even if wish ... the truth can be grasped as if pictures on paper with the aid of a machine' (GM i. 84). What Leibniz is doing here is getting rid of the need to reflect on each step in a proof by making one's traversal of these steps not instantaneous, as was

Descartes's solution, but mechanical, something which requires no thought yet compels intellectual assent. Moreover, Leibniz, apparently taking it as given that we cannot say anything about cognitive processes different from ours, proceeds to ascribe to God a reasoning process modelled upon our own. We can have an understanding of God's grasp of truth because we can provide a mechanical model for such a grasp.[45] Before we can explore this issue, however, we need to examine the very different roles that Descartes and Leibniz give to algebra, and to analysis and synthesis.

[45] The idea of modelling God on human beings is not peculiar to his logic. It is a characteristic feature of his account of ethics and politics also, where God effectively functions as a philosopher-king. Cf. S. Brown, *Leibniz* (Sussex, 1984), 191.

3

Discovery and Proof

DESCARTES'S construal of inference in terms of an instantaneous grasp in accord with the natural light of reason precludes any attempt to provide a formal account of logical relations, since any such attempt would of necessity focus on inferential steps, and this is precisely what Descartes's account is designed to take us away from. Yet throughout his work Descartes thinks of true and effective reasoning in terms of mathematical reasoning, and mathematical reasoning is, for him, algebraic reasoning. Algebraic reasoning is formal, indeed it is the paradigm of formal reasoning, and the beginnings of modern logic can be traced back to Boole's representation of the theorems of traditional syllogistic in algebraic terms. How can Descartes hold up algebra as a model on the one hand, and deride attempts to provide a formal account of inference on the other?

Our task in this chapter is to determine to what extent two apparently antithetical ideas, the *intuitus* conception of inference and the algebraic conception of reasoning, can be reconciled. The key to the problem lies in Descartes's construal of algebra as a method of discovery, and in the way he distinguishes between a method of discovery and a method of presentation. Syllogistic, and deductive reasoning generally, he sees as coming in the latter category. Consequently, there is a sharp division set up between algebraic reasoning and deductive inference. Our concern will be with how this sharp division comes about, and what consequences it has.

ANALYSIS AND DISCOVERY

In the *Reply to the Second Set of Objections*, Descartes give his reasons for not propounding his arguments 'in a geometrical fashion' in terms of a distinction between 'the order and the method of proof' (AT vii. 155 ff.). The geometrical order of proof consists simply in presenting one's material in such a way that one is always able to explain that material in terms of what has gone before. Descartes tells us that he tries to follow the geometrical order of proof in the *Meditations*, and this has required that he present the mind/body distinction in the *Sixth Meditation* and not in the *Second*. The point of this remark is presumably that, were it not for these considerations of order of presentation, we might expect such a fundamental and important distinction to be presented as early as the *Second Meditation*.[1]

The geometrical method of proof involves two procedures, analysis and synthesis. Analysis shows us 'the way in which something has been methodically discovered' and in following an analytic proof carefully we have a full understanding of what is proved, as much as if we ourselves had discovered it. As Descartes puts it, 'we make the conclusion our own'. Such a mode of proof does not compel assent, however, for it will fail to convince someone who is inattentive, a grasp of all the parts of the proof being necessary for a grasp of the necessity of the conclusion. Nor, he adds, will it convince someone who is hostile. Finally, some things are scarcely touched upon in analysis even when they are important, namely those things that are clear in themselves. Synthesis, on the other hand, proceeds 'in the opposite direction'. It clearly demonstrates conclusions in a way that compels assent from everyone. Yet it is not as satisfying to those eager to learn, we are told, because it does not show the way in which what is being taught was discovered. Synthesis, however, was alone used by ancient geometers, who wanted to keep their analytic method to themselves. Having distinguished analysis and synthesis in this

[1] On this issue see B. Williams, *Descartes* (Harmondsworth, 1978), 105 ff.

way, Descartes goes on to point out in the *Meditations* he has used only analysis. Synthesis is appropriate after one has carried out analysis in geometry, but not in metaphysics. The reason is that 'the primary notions that are taken as given [i.e. as axioms] in geometrical proofs are in agreement with sense experience and are generally conceded by all'. The only thing that remains to be done in such cases is 'the proper deduction of consequences'. This, Descartes maintains, 'may be performed by anyone, even the least attentive, provided that one remembers what has gone before; and the detailed division of propositions is designed so that they might be easily remembered and hence so that people will be made to remember even if they are unwilling'. In metaphysics, on the other hand, the most difficult task is to establish the clarity and distinctness of its primary notions, something which is hampered by our reliance on our senses, and which requires that we withdraw our mind as far as possible from corporeal matters.

The meaning of the terms 'analysis' and 'synthesis' is, however, much less clear than this account might lead us to believe. Since a good deal hinges on Descartes's usage of the terms, our first concern must be to clarify how he understands them. At the beginning of the *Reply to the Second Set of Objections*, Descartes associates them with a priori and a posteriori discovery, but this turns out to be utterly unhelpful (cf. Appendix to this chapter). Of more help is their association with the traditional notions of resolution and composition. In Commandino's 1589 Latin edition of Pappus, the Greek mathematical terms ἀνάλυσις and σύνθεσις are translated as *resolutio* and *compositio* respectively.[2] But these latter are broader philosophical terms having a different origin. The distinction between resolution, also known as *demonstratio quia*, and composition, also known as *demonstratio propter quid*, goes back to one in Aristotle that we have already looked at, that between demonstration of fact (τοῦ ὅτι) and scientific demonstration (τοῦ διότι) respectively. The former is that where the proximate cause (the planets' being near) is demonstrated from

---

[2] See N. W. Gilbert, *Renaissance Concepts of Method* (New York, 1960), 82.

the phenomenon to which it gives rise (the planets' not twinkling), whereas the latter is that where a sensible phenomenon (the
planets' not twinkling) is demonstrated from its proximate cause
(the planets' being near). In the Galenic tradition, the two
procedures are combined. Because in this tradition syllogistic
(backed up by inductive and classificatory procedures) was taken
to provide a method of discovery as well as a method of demonstration, one kind of syllogistic procedure was needed to find the
fundamental principles or causes, and another to demonstrate that
these indeed were what one claimed them to be. Consequently,
what we must do is first to perform a demonstration *quia*, in which
we move inferentially from cause to effect, and then a demonstration *propter quid*, in which we move inferentially from the cause so
discovered to the effect. There is an appearance of circularity here
of course, in that our procedure involves inference from effect to
cause to effect. The *regressus* theories of the sixteenth century
provided the most developed response to this problem by attempting to show that the type of knowledge of an effect that we start
with (sensory knowledge) is different in kind from the type of
knowledge of the effect that we have at the end of the demonstration (knowledge in terms of a proximate cause).[3] Leaving to one
side this question of the qualitative transformation of knowledge,
however, the project can be seen in broad terms as involving two
types of inference: an inference to the best explanation, and then
an attempt to show that that explanation is indeed the true one
by showing how the appropriate consequences can be inferred
from it.

There are undeniable similarities between resolution and composition on the one hand, and analysis and synthesis on the other.
Analysis and synthesis form a unified procedure in Greek
mathematics. Pappus calls analysis a 'solution backwards', while in
synthesis we suppose 'what has been reached last in analysis, and

---

[3] The real problem for accounts of this kind was to distinguish, from amongst the many
constant concomitants of an effect, its proximate cause. On this question, see N. Jardine,
'Galileo's Road of Truth and the Demonstrative Regress', *Studies in History and Philosophy
of Science*, 7 (1976), 277–318.

arranging in their natural order as consequents the former antecedents and linking them with one another, we in the end arrive at
the construction of the thing sought'.[4] Pappus distinguishes two
kinds of analysis: 'theoretical analysis', in which we attempt to
establish the truth of theorems, and 'problematical analysis', in
which we aim to find something that is unknown. Analysis starts
with the problem or theorem to be shown, and proceeds via
constituent problems or theorems (ἀνάλυσις literally means an
'untying') until one of two things is achieved. The first kind of
thing that can happen is that we come across a negative result: in
the case of theoretical analysis, we reach something false, or in the
case of problematical analysis we reach something impossible to
construct, so the problem is insoluble. In these cases, there can be
no synthesis, the analysis being complete in itself. The second kind
of thing that can happen is that analysis can lead us to a theorem or
theorems which we know to be true, or which we are familiar with,
and so on, or it can lead us to questions which are well understood,
which we know how to solve, and so forth. Note that it is not just a
question of analysis leading us to something which we know to be
true. Analysis is a heuristic procedure and there can be no prior
specification of exactly what the analysis will come to an end at:
this will depend on a number of factors, not least how familiar the
person performing the analysis is with the kinds of questions being
dealt with. One thing that is clear, however, is that we need
synthesis to complete the analysis in such cases. The problem is
what this synthesis amounts to: what does synthesis actually do?
Although the question is a disputed one, the evidence militates
strongly against the view that analysis and synthesis were methods
of proof in antiquity.[5] Proof in ancient mathematics would have

---

[4] Text and translation can be found in J. Hintikka and U. Remes, *The Method of Analysis* (Dordrecht, 1974), 8–10.

[5] Hintikka and Remes (*The Method of Analysis*) defend the idea that analysis is a method of finding theorems and synthesis a way of proving them, the two procedures forming a unified method of proof analysable in strictly logical terms. This view is successfully challenged, and the idea that they make up a heuristic procedure defended, in A. Szabó's 'Working Backwards and Proving by Synthesis', which appears as Appendix I in Hintikka and Remes, *The Method of Analysis*, and in more detail in his 'Analysis und Synthesis', *Acta classica*, 10/11 (1974/5), 155–64. See also the blunt but informative rebuttal by E. Maula in his 'An End of Invention', *Annals of Science*, 38 (1981), 109–22.

followed one or other of the traditional procedures: the Eleatic method of indirect proof, the Eudoxean method of exhaustion, geometrical construction, algoristic method, and so on. Such procedures would usually be employed within synthesis, but they are not constitutive of synthesis.

The function of synthesis is twofold, depending on whether it follows a theoretical or a problematical analysis. As I have indicated, in the case of both theoretical and problematical analyses with negative results there is no place for synthesis. The analysis provides a *reductio ad contradictionem* or a *reductio ad absurdum* and is a complete demonstration in its own right. In the case of a positive result in theoretical analysis, that positive result is achieved when we show that a true theorem (q) follows from (i.e. can be 'unwound' from) the theorem (p) whose truth we wish to establish. As Aristotle puts it, 'if it were impossible to prove truth from falsehood, analysis would be easy, for they would convert from necessity' (*An. Post.* A12, 78^a 6–7). That is, given the truth of q, we would be able to establish $q \supset p$ and hence $p \equiv q$ from $p \supset q$, just as easily as we can establish $\neg p$ from showing that $p \supset \neg q$. But of course we can sometimes derive truths from falsehoods, so we need synthesis to show that $q \supset p$. This is in fact the 'natural order' for Pappus and Greek mathematicians generally, the analysis being only a 'solution backwards'. So what we are almost invariably presented with are the 'naturally ordered' synthetic demonstrations: there is no need to present the analysis as well.

The case of problematical analysis with a positive outcome is a bit more complicated, for here there is an extra reason why synthesis is needed. Analysis in Greek mathematics concerns general procedure whereas synthesis, as Klein has pointed out, is required for the synthetic realization of this procedure in what he calls a 'univocally determinate object'.[6] In the case of geometry this is a geometrical figure. But similar constraints held in arithmetic also. Arithmetical analysis yields only an indeterminate solution, and we need a final synthetic stage corresponding to the geometrical construction; this is the numerical exploitation of the indeterminate solution, where we compute determinate numbers. Since in his *Geometry* Descartes will be concerned almost exclusively with problematical analysis and since he will reject the need for synthesis altogether, the question of this perceived extra need for synthesis is worth looking at a bit more closely.

Consider what was the most influential account of number as far as Greek and Alexandrian mathematicians were concerned, that of Aristotle. In the later books of the *Metaphysics*, Aristotle provides a philosophical basis for the Greek conception of number.[7] An aspect of Aristotle's account which is at first sight puzzling is the fact that he makes general statements about mathematics on a number of occasions and proceeds to fill them out exclusively in terms of apparently geometrical considerations, as if this were sufficient to cover arithmetic also. In discussing the intelligible matter of mathematical objects, for example, he distinguishes between sensible figures and numbers and intelligible or noetic figures and numbers (a distinction common to all Greek philosophical discussions of geometry and arithmetic), and maintains that all mathematical objects have intelligible matter. He then proceeds to describe the abstract spatial dimensions of geometrical figures. We are given no separate indication of what the intelligible matter of numbers might be. On the other hand, Aristotle makes a sharp distinction between arithmetic and geometry, and they cannot be identified. It turns out, however, that in giving us an account of the intelligible matter of geometrical figures Aristotle is in fact also giving us an account of the intelligible matter of numbers, and in a way that respects the distinction between the two. The distinction is formulated in terms of two divisions of the category of quantity: plurality ($\pi\lambda\hat{\eta}\theta\circ\varsigma$), which is potentially divisible into discontinuous or discrete parts, and spatial magnitude ($\mu\acute{\epsilon}\gamma\epsilon\theta\circ\varsigma$), which is potentially divisible into continuous parts (*Metaph.* E, 1020[a] 7 ff.).

---

[7] For the detailed arguments lying behind what follows in this paragraph see my 'Aristotle on Intelligible Matter', *Phronesis*, 25 (1980), 187–97, and 'The One and the Many: Aristotle on the Individuation of Numbers', *Classical Quarterly*, NS 22 (1982), 312–22, which deals with a closely related topic.

The line, for example, is divisible into continuous parts in the sense that it is infinitely divisible (*Ph.* VI 2, 232^b 24 and *Cael.* II, 268^a 7, 29), so numbers cannot be conceived as lines. But they can be construed as line *lengths*. Line lengths are lines, but they are lines measured by some specific unit length (*Metaph.* I, 1052^b 31–3) and it is in virtue of being so 'measured' that they are numbers, numbers being defined as pluralities 'measured' by a 'one' (1057^a 3–4). The noetic or abstract line length, in so far as it is a determinate length, is potentially divisible into discontinuous or discrete parts, that is into a determinate plurality of unit lengths, and this is exactly what noetic numbers are. Hence it is not surprising that Aristotle's arithmetical terminology—*linear*, *plane*, and *solid* numbers, numbers being *measured*, factors *measuring* products in multiplication—has a geometrical ring to it. The point is that, although one is dealing with lines and planes, and so on, because one is treating these arithmetically one is dealing with them not *qua* lines and planes but *qua* unit lengths and unit areas, or sums or products of such unit lengths and areas. When Aristotle, and Greek and Alexandrian mathematicians generally, talk of numbers in one dimension, plane numbers and solid numbers, they mean what they say. Geometry does not merely provide the notation for arithmetic, and no Greek or Alexandrian author ever talks of numbers being *represented* geometrically. Arithmetical propositions (see, for example, Books 7 to 9 of Euclid's *Elements*) are stated in terms of line lengths not because this is how numbers are represented but because this is what they are.

This is an extraordinarily constrictive conception of arithmetic. Consider the arithmetical operation of multiplication and, in particular, the dimensional change involved in this operation, so that the product is always of a higher dimension. On the Greek and Alexandrian interpretation, for example, if a is a line length, a^2 is a square having sides of length a, ab is a rectangle having sides of lengths a and b, and a^3 is a cube having sides of length a. This is not a notational constraint, it is inherently connected with the idea that numbers are always numbers *of* something. Consequently, when we multiply, we must multiply numbers of something: we cannot multiply two by three, we must multiply two somethings by three somethings. Moreover, not only are the dimensional aspects of geometry retained in arithmetical operations, so too is the physical and intuitive nature of these dimensions so that, for example, no more than three lengths can be multiplied together since the product here is a solid, which exhausts the number of available dimensions.[8]

Descartes does not employ synthesis in his *Geometry*; he can get by quite happily without it. Consider the traditional need for synthesis to establish the biconditional. Descartes's analytic procedure involves the reduction of problems to simultaneous equations for which solution-procedures are known or discoverable:

Thus if we want to solve any problem, it should first be considered as if we already had the solution and [letters assigned] to all the lines, whether known or unknown, that appear to be needed for the construction of the solution. Then, making no distinction between known and unknown lines, we should go over the difficulty in the way that shows most naturally the relation between these lines, until we can express a single quantity in two ways. This we call an equation, for the terms of one of these two expressions are together equal to the terms of the other. (AT vi. 372.)

We are dealing here with equations, and all equalities are automatically reversible, so there is no problem of valid converses, and hence no need for synthesis on these grounds. In general, to obtain a synthetic demonstration of a proposition so discovered we need only reverse the analysis.[9] The synthetic proof of Descartes's solution to Pappus' locus-problem for four or more lines, for

---

[8] The only exception I know of to this constraint in the whole of the Greek and Alexandrian corpus occurs in a relatively late Alexandrian work, Heron's *Metrica*, I. 8, where two squares (i.e. areas) are multiplied together. One scholiast on the *Metrica* regards it as an oversight on Heron's part. Whether this is the case or not, it is certainly not something Heron could have justified: his result is unconstructible in Alexandrian terms.

[9] There are rare exceptions here, one of the most notable being the kind of demonstration involved in Fermat's mature method of quadrature, for example, where infinitesimals and limit procedures are employed for which there was no corresponding synthetic procedure available at the time. Cf. M. Mahoney, *The Mathematical Career of Pierre de Fermat* (Princeton, 1973), 47–8.

example, is given by simply going through the analysis backwards. But what would the point of such an exercise be? The analysis not only yields the result but shows one, in a way that is generalizable, how the result is achieved. Synthesis now begins to look quite artificial and its value obscure.

We find in the *Geometry* no lists of definitions, postulates, and so on, and no theorems demonstrated. The first book of the *Geometry* opens with a direct comparison between arithmetic and geometry. Arithmetic, we are told, consists in the operations of addition, subtraction, multiplication, division, and finding roots, and geometrical problems can all be reduced to a problem in which all we seek is the length of a straight line. The two sets of operations are then combined, arithmetical procedures being directly introduced into geometry, thereby developing exceptionally powerful problem-solving devices. Multiplication, for example, is an operation in which, traditionally, a rectangle is constructed from two line segments. This is a procedure that Descartes himself followed in his earlier writings (before about 1630), but in the *Geometry* he completely transcends it: multiplication is an operation which can be performed using only straight lines:

Let AB be taken as one unit, [see Fig. 1] and let it be required to multiply BD by BC. I have only to join the points A and C, and draw DE parallel to CA; then BE is the product of this multiplication. (AT vi. 370.)

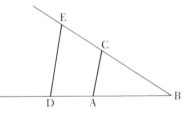

If we wish to find a square root, on the other hand, we require straight lines and circles:

In order to find the square root of GH, [see Fig. 2] I add, along the straight line, FG equal to one unit; then, dividing FH into two equal

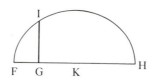

parts at K, I describe the circle FIH around K as a centre, and draw from the point G a straight line at right angles to G extended to I, and GI is the required root. (AT vi. 370–1.)

Descartes next introduces single letters to designate line lengths, but his interpretation of these is significantly different from the traditional one. Products and powers have the same number of dimensions as everything else: the line length is freed almost completely from spatial intuitions,[10] and dimensional homogeneity is explicitly introduced:

It should be noted that all the parts of a single line should always be expressed by the same number of dimensions as one another, provided that the unit is not determined in the condition of the problem. Thus, a^3 contains as many dimensions as ab^2 or b^3, these being the component parts of the line that I have called $3\sqrt{a^3 - b^3 + b^2}$. (AT vi. 371.)

The development of these tools is a crucial ingredient in the analytic process. Once he has presented them, Descartes takes us straight to the heart of one of the great unsolved problems of antiquity, Pappus' locus-problem for four or more lines. The four-line problem as Pappus presents it is this: starting with four lines in given positions, find the locus of points from which four lines can be drawn to the four given lines, each making a given angle with it, such that the product of the length of two of the lines bears a constant proportion to the product of the other two. Pappus (following Apollonius of Perga) knew that the locus is a conic section, but, Descartes maintains, was unable to describe or explain the locus in cases of four or more lines. Descartes's techniques, which amongst other things are not constrained by

---

[10] The only spatial element still active in Descartes's conception of number is the spatial intuition behind his idea of the continuum of real numbers, something that was not to be questioned until well into the 19th cent.

considerations of the dimension of the product, enable us, he argues, to solve this problem for any number of lines. In fact he cannot show this, and his techniques are not quite sufficient to provide a catalogue of cubics, quartics, quintics, and so on, which is what would be required.[11] They are, nevertheless, immensely more powerful than anything available in antiquity. But there is also a very significant difference in approach between the mathematicians of antiquity and Descartes. Descartes's concern is not with rigorous proof, but with developing techniques for solving problems. This, for him, is constitutive of analysis, and ultimately of mathematics.

In traditional terms, the *Geometry* is an exercise in problematical analysis. What then of the traditional requirement that, following such an analysis, synthesis is needed to construct or compute a determinate figure or number? For mathematicians of antiquity this was the point of the exercise. It was only if such a determinate figure or number could be constructed or computed that one could be said to have solved the problem. Moreover, the only numbers allowable as solutions were natural numbers: negative numbers in particular were 'impossible' numbers. Towards the end of the Alexandrian period, most notably in Diophantus' *Arithmetica*, we begin to find a search for problems and solutions concerned with general magnitudes, but these procedures never make up anything more than auxiliary techniques forming a stage preliminary to the final one, where a determinate number is computed.[12] Descartes's approach is completely contrary to this. As early as Rule 16 of the *Regulae* he spells out the contrast between his procedure and the traditional one:

It must be pointed out that while arithmeticians have usually designated each magnitude by several units, i.e. by a number, we on the contrary abstract from numbers themselves here just as we did above [Rule 14] from geometrical figures, or from anything else. Our reason for doing this is partly to avoid the tedium of a long and unnecessary calculation, but

[11] See E. Grosholz, 'Descartes' Unification of Algebra and Geometry', in S. Gaukroger (ed.), *Descartes* (Sussex, 1980), 156–68.
[12] See J. Klein, *Greek Mathematical Thought*, pp. 133 ff.

mainly to see that those parts of the problem which are the essential ones always remain distinct and are not obscured by useless numbers. If for example we are trying to find the hypotenuse of a right-angled triangle whose given sides are 9 and 12, the arithmetician will say that it is $\sqrt{225}$, i.e. 15. We on the other hand will write a and b for 9 and 12, and find that the hypotenuse is $\sqrt{a^2+b^2}$, leaving the two parts of the expression, a^2 and b^2, distinct, whereas in the number they are run together ... We who seek to develop a clear and distinct knowledge of these things insist on these distinctions. Arithmeticians, on the other hand, are satisfied if the required result turns up, even if they do not see how it depends on what has been given, but in fact it is in knowledge of this kind alone that science consists. (AT x. 455–6, 458.)

In sum, for Descartes concern with general magnitudes is constitutive of the mathematical enterprise. Moreover, he recognizes no numbers and figures to be 'impossible' on intuitive or other grounds: his algebra is the only thing that constrains what is possible. Not only are numbers of any power allowed, and dimensional changes ruled out, but Descartes accedes to purely algebraic constraints requiring that 'number' be extended to include not just integers, but fractions and irrationals as well. Most remarkable of all, he is prepared to allow, so as to preserve the generality of his structural analysis of the equation, not only negative roots, despite the fact that he is ill at ease with these,[13] but also imaginary roots, even though on any independent grounds these are completely counterintuitive. Not only do we no longer need to supplement analysis with the synthetic computation of number, but analysis has now become so self-sufficient that it actually tells us what is going to count as a number.

In sum, the two traditional reasons for the necessity of synthesis in mathematics are rejected by Descartes, and with some justification: his own algebra transcends the need either to establish converses or to solve a problem by computing a determinate number. But to reject the traditional need for synthesis in mathematics is one thing, to reject deduction is quite another. In Rule 4 of the *Regulae*, where he first makes his complaint about

[13] See J. F. Scott, *The Scientific Work of René Descartes* (London, 1976), 141.

Pappus and Diophantus keeping their method of discovery secret, he tells us that they put in the place of analysis 'sterile truths' which they 'demonstrated deductively' (AT x. 376). What makes these truths sterile, and what makes the truths revealed by analysis fertile? It cannot be due to any difference in the necessity of the conclusions, for there is none. In synthesis we 'clearly demonstrate the conclusions' and these conclusions 'can be shown to be contained in what has gone before' (AT vii. 156), and in the case of analysis he notes that if the least thing escapes our attention then 'the necessity of the conclusion is lost' (AT vii. 155–6), that is, the conclusion is in fact necessary when this does not occur. In the mathematical case, the thrust of the argument seems to be that, if we have shown something once (in analysis), why show it a second time (in synthesis), especially since all we would be doing would be reversing the demonstration already given? But the problem is what 'show' amounts to here. Leaving to one side (for consideration in the next chapter) what 'show' means in the extra-mathematical case of resolution and composition (and analysis and synthesis construed extra-mathematically), the problem is that Descartes appears to imply that in analysis we show things non-deductively, whereas in synthesis we show them deductively, and that the former is superior.

Analysis cannot be superior because its inferences lend themselves to being grasped in an *intuitus* more readily than do those of synthesis. Indeed, quite the contrary appears to be the case. Consider the question why, if in analysis the conclusion is necessary, it nevertheless does not always compel assent. Two obstacles to the compulsion of its arguments are given: lack of attention and hostility. Lack of attention precludes one grasping the necessity of the conclusion of an analytic demonstration because in order to do this one must grasp all the steps. 'Hostility' turns out to be a related phenomenon. Synthetic proofs overcome lack of attention by arranging the steps in such a way that they cannot be forgotten. But such proofs also apparently overcome hostility in that 'hostile readers', being aware of all the steps because the nature of synthetic presentation makes it impossible not to remember them ('even against their will'), cannot reject the conclusion. In short, synthesis is constituted in such a way as to be an aid to memory. This is the only positive characteristic that Descartes ascribes to it. Even so, would not this in itself make it preferable to analysis? On Descartes's account, in both analysis and synthesis we need to be aware of all the steps if we are to grasp the necessity of the conclusion. Synthesis presents the steps in such a way that no one can fail to be aware of them. Analysis does not. Consequently, it would appear that synthesis lends itself much more easily to the intuitive grasp that is ultimately constitutive of inference. After all, we have to see the steps and their connections clearly before we can go through them so quickly that we grasp the connection between the premises and conclusion in the one intuition.

The point remains, however, that synthesis only yields 'sterile truths'. The thinking behind Descartes's characterization of truths demonstrated synthetically/deductively as sterile is presumably that whereas in analysis we are discovering new truths, in synthesis we are merely rearranging already known truths. In this respect, his conception of synthesis bears a striking resemblance to his conception of an artificial language, set out in a letter to Mersenne of 20 November 1629:

Nevertheless, I believe that one could in addition invent a system in which it would be possible to learn the primitive words and their characters in the language very quickly and by means of an order, i.e. by establishing an order among all the thoughts that can come into the human mind just like that which is naturally established among numbers. And just as one can learn in one day to name all the numbers right up to infinity and to write them, in an unknown language, so too the same might be done with all the other things that come into the human mind. . . . The discovery of such a language depends on the True Philosophy, for without it it is impossible to number and order the thoughts of men, or even to sort them out into clear and distinct ideas, which to my mind is the great secret for acquiring the true Science. And if someone were to give a correct account of what are the simple ideas in the human imagination out of which is composed everything that they think, and if this account were generally accepted, I would then dare to hope for a universal language which was very easy to learn, speak and write. Most of all, such a language would assist our judgment by representing matters so clearly that it would be almost impossible to go wrong. As it is, almost all our words have confused meanings, and men's minds have become so accustomed to them that there is virtually nothing that they can understand perfectly. Now I hold that such a language is possible, and that the Science on which it depends can be discovered. It would make peasants better able to judge the truth about the world than philosophers now are. But do not hope ever to see such a language in use. For that, the natural order would have to change so much that the world would have to become a terrestrial paradise, and this only happens in fiction. (AT i. 81–2.)

Here is described something which, were it practicable, would present truths to us in a completely compelling way, but it depends on our first having discovered the 'true philosophy'. Its role is almost indistinguishable from that of synthesis. It enables truths to be arranged in such a way that the systematic connection between them can be displayed. They can then be presented clearly and distinctly, which means that they would automatically compel assent. But what we are displaying a systematic connection between here are already known truths: a universal language cannot, any more than synthesis, produce new truths.

Here we face what, I suggest, is a fundamental problem in Descartes's account. His procedure in algebra leads him to reject synthesis and he generalizes this to a wholesale rejection of deduction. But in fact algebraic considerations provide the key to a proper understanding of deduction. Even if we were to accept that in synthesis we are doing something that produces no new truths (bearing in mind the various rather different things, outlined in Chapter 1, that could be meant by the demand for 'new truths'), in fact even if we grant that deduction is trivial in the sense that the truths we deduce are already contained in those we started off with, is it not still important to know what follows (even if trivially) from what, and what does not, and why? In raising the question of the standing of deduction we are raising a question about the systematic connections between truths. We are not concerned just with the particular content of those truths. The situation bears an analogy to mathematics. Descartes tells us on a number of occasions that, in contrast to earlier mathematicians, he is not concerned with computing particular numerical solutions to equations, but rather with structural features of the equations themselves. He is concerned with the systematic relations between general magnitudes symbolized in algebraic equations. But are not particular numbers somewhat like particular truths here?: can we not explore the relations between truths simply *qua* truths in a correspondingly abstract way by abstracting from particular truths? Descartes sees the distinguishing feature of his approach as lying in the fact that he abstracts from numbers. Can we not similarly abstract from particular truths and, analogously, explore the relation between them in abstract terms? Descartes does not raise these questions. He decides that, because deduction cannot be productive of new truths, it follows that the relation between truths that it establishes is regulated merely by presentational considerations, although the only presentational advantage he can find in synthesis is a mnemonic one. But of course this does not follow, and had he made the move to a higher level of abstraction, a move he makes so brilliantly in the case of geometry and arithmetic, this would, I believe, have become evident.

Descartes held in his own work on algebra the key to a profound and new understanding of the nature of deduction, but he did not recognize it. Leibniz did, and a comparison with Leibniz's approach will enable us to see in more detail the exact nature of the questions at issue here.

SYNTHESIS AND PROOF

Leibniz had distinctive views on both the role and nature of deduction which differ radically from those of Descartes. Like Descartes, he is concerned with the nature of algebra, and with the role of analysis and synthesis. But whereas this concern leads

Descartes to identify deduction with synthesis conceived as a procedure for presentation of truths rather than the discovery of truths, for Leibniz the identification of deduction and synthesis leads him to think of them in terms of a method of discovery; and indeed as something even more general and abstract than algebra.

Let us focus to begin with on the issue of how Leibniz can construe synthesis as a method of discovery. In *On Universal Synthesis and Analysis* (GP vii. 292–8), Leibniz explicitly denies the claim that analysis 'consists in revealing the origin of a discovery' whereas synthesis conceals it. Analysis, we are told, is of value in solving problems, but this is really the limit of its usefulness. Synthesis, on the other hand, is a means of discovering and solving new problems. It consists in the ordering of truths, 'discovering certain progressions', and letting new and important questions emerge from these. In a letter to Gabriel Wagner in 1696 he tells us that, provided one starts from a reasonable store of information, one can survey it and uncover an order in it, and once this order is discerned it enables us to go on to discover many new things (GP vii. 523). Synthesis is explicitly conceived as a method of discovery, and the general thrust of the argument is that analysis is concerned merely with the solution of given problems, whereas in synthesis we set in train a systematic structuring of and extension of knowledge which enables gaps, difficulties, flaws, and so on to be recognized, precisely identified, and solved (either analytically or synthetically). The contrast with Descartes is stark. Descartes's *Geometry* is concerned exclusively with problem-solving: for Descartes this is constitutive of mathematics, as opposed to the barren synthetic procedures of the ancients. For Leibniz, the point of the exercise is not problem-solving but rather the systematic extension of knowledge, and this can only be achieved synthetically.

Leibniz's commitment to the value of synthesis goes beyond a commitment to its heuristic value in systematically extending our knowledge, however. In the *Nouveaux Essais* he raises a question about proof in arithmetic that goes right to the core of his rejection of the idea that deductive or synthetic demonstrations show nothing. He is specifically concerned with Locke here, of course, but the issue is one that affects Descartes equally. Locke had maintained in the *Essay* (IV. vii. 10), in the context of discussing purported first principles of knowledge, that 'these magnified maxims' as he calls them 'are not the principles or foundations of all our other knowledge'. He continues:

For if there be a great many other truths, which have as much self-evidence as they, and a great many that we know before them, it is impossible that they should be the principles from which we deduce all other truths. Is it impossible to know that one and two are equal to three, but by virtue of this, or some other such maxim, viz. 'the whole is equal to all its parts taken together'? Many a one knows that one and two are equal to three, without having heard, or thought on, that or any other axiom by which it might be proved; and knows it as certainly as any other maxim; and all from the same reason of self-evidence ... Nor after the knowledge, that the whole is equal to all its parts, does he know that one and two are equal to three, better or more certainly than he did before.

Leibniz replies by maintaining that $2+2=4$ is 'not quite an immediate truth'. It can be demonstrated, and he demonstrates it. We assume first that 4 'signifies' $3+1$, and then define 2, 3, and 4 as follows:

Def. 1: $2 = 1 + 1$
Def. 2: $3 = 2 + 1$
Def. 3: $4 = 3 + 1$

We then assume, as an axiom, that identicals can be substituted for one another (Leibniz's Law). The demonstration is then provided, and can be presented as follows:

$2+2=2+2$	Substitution, Leibniz's Law	(1)
$2+2=2+(1+1)$	By Def. 1	(2)
$2+2=(2+1)+1$	(Tacit assumption of associativity of addition)	(3)
$2+2=3+1$	By Def. 2	(4)
$2+2=4$	By Def. 3	(5)

What does such a demonstration show? It does not show that someone who is not familiar with the demonstration does not, or cannot, know that $2+2=4$. Nor does knowledge of the demonstration enable us to be more certain of the truth of $2+2=4$ than we could be were we not familiar with it. Both of these would be absurd, and Leibniz's demonstration does nothing to rebut Locke's views on these matters. Another alternative is that it shows that $2+2=4$ is not self-evident at all, or at least not completely self-evident or as self-evident as we might have thought. At least one commentator has maintained this,[14] and it does apparently accord with Leibniz's remark that $2+2=4$ 'is not quite an immediate truth'. But such a claim would be ridiculous, for on what grounds could it be maintained that $2=1+1$ or $4=3+1$ are more self-evident than $2+2=4$? The point of the demonstration cannot be to show less self-evident from more self-evident principles, for the degree of self-evidence is surely the same. If this were what Leibniz were trying to show, Descartes and Locke would be completely vindicated.

If we are to understand what the demonstration shows we must not run together questions of self-evidence and questions of truth. Leibniz has Philalethes concede that while the demonstration is unnecessary, it nevertheless shows how the truth of $2+2=4$ depends on axioms and definitions. The demonstration is unnecessary, I suggest, in the sense that one does not need to know the demonstration in order to know the truth of the proposition that $2+2=4$. One knows its truth because it is self-evident. However, while the self-evidence of the proposition does not depend on the demonstration, its truth does. Its truth depends on the demonstration in the sense that $2+2=4$ is true if and only if $2=1+1$, $3=2+1$, and $4=3+1$ are true, and if Leibniz's Law (and the associativity of addition) holds. The distinction between truth and self-evidence is crucial to Leibniz's project. What lies behind the conceptions of Descartes and Locke is the idea that if a truth is

<hr/>

[14] See J. Gibson, *Locke's Theory of Knowledge and its Historical Relations* (Cambridge, 1931), 297. In the main, commentators are surprisingly silent about what the demonstration actually shows.

self-evident then it is misguided to imagine that one could demonstrate it, for to do this one would have to account for it in terms of something more evident, but a self-evident truth is as evident as can be. Leibniz's demonstration, however, in no way depends on the fact that $2 + 2 = 4$ is self-evident: the demonstration would go through even if it were not at all evident. What matters is the systematic connection between this truth and others. Two propositions may be equally self-evident yet the truth of one may presuppose and not be presupposed by the truth of the other. What Locke has assumed is that if something is a self-evident truth it is an independent truth. Leibniz's demonstration shows that this is not the case. Its self-evidence does not depend on anything else—this is, after all, what 'self-evident' means—but its truth may well do so.

This form of demonstration is clearly not restricted to arithmetic, and Leibniz has an exceptionally broad conception of its purview. 'Common algebra', he writes in *On Universal Synthesis and Analysis*, is concerned only with quantities or equalities and inequalities, whereas what he calls 'the art of combinations' or 'general characteristic' deals with the 'form or formulas of things in general, i.e. *quality* in general or similarity or dissimilarity' (GP vii. 298). Yet what he is seeking is not merely a very abstract form of algebra but one with universal scope. As he puts it in the Preface to his *General Science*, 'it is clear that if one could find characters or symbols suited to expressing all our thoughts as clearly and accurately as arithmetic expresses numbers or geometry expresses lines, one would obviously be able to do with everything *which is subject to reasoning* what one does in arithmetic and geometry' (C p. 155). What Leibniz is concerned with here is a universal language, but his conception of this universal language differs from Descartes's in that, whereas Descartes saw the project in terms of a notation which aided communication of already-established truths, Leibniz conceives of it as an instrument of discovery. In a letter to Nicolas Remond of 10 January 1714, he imagines a *spécieuse générale* in which all truths of reason are reduced to a calculus, and this would, he writes, be a new universal language, 'for the characters and words themselves would give directions to reason, and errors (except errors of fact) would only be mistakes in calculation' (GP iii. 606). In sum, Leibniz's project is to establish not a language which merely displays the logical relations between already-known truths, but a language whose operations lead us to new truths.

These operations constitute the issue on which Descartes's and Leibniz's conceptions of inference part company most radically. Descartes does envisage a quasi-mechanical procedure by which reasoning might take place when, in his discussion of an artificial or universal language, he talks of 'establishing an order among all the thoughts that can come into the human mind just like that which is naturally established among numbers', but such a procedure, as we have seen, is not able to produce any new truths, and in any case is not practicable in his opinion. This view is worth comparing with Hobbes's. Hobbes had explicitly construed reasoning in terms of mathematical computation in his *Elements of Philosophy* (*De corpore*). At the beginning of the first part, entitled 'Computation or Logic', he writes:

PHILOSOPHY *is such knowledge of effects or appearances, as we acquire by true ratiocination from the knowledge we have first of their causes or generation; And again, of such causes or generations as may be from knowing first their effects* ... By RATIOCINATION, I mean *computation*. Now to compute, is either to collect the sum of many things that are added together, or to know what remains when one thing is taken out of another. *Ratiocination*, therefore, is the same with *addition* and *substraction*; and if any man add *multiplication* and *division*, I will not be against it, seeing multiplication is nothing but addition of equals to one another, and division is nothing but a substraction of equals from one another, as often as is possible. So that all ratiocination is comprehended in these two operations of the mind, addition and substraction. (EW i. 3.)

Hobbes then goes on to give an example. Knowing that man is a rational animal and that an animal is an animated body, we can form the equation:

$$body + animated + rational = man$$

and from this we can obtain another expression:

$$man - rational = animated + body$$

But such 'computational' procedures are not productive of new truths, and they depend upon a prior classification of the elements of the universe. This is the real task in Hobbes's project, just as it was for Descartes, and just as it was in the most developed artificial or universal language proposed in the seventeenth century, John Wilkins's *Essay Towards a Real Character and a Philosophical Language*, the great bulk of which consists in a painstaking and tedious 'enumeration of things and notions'.

But there is another respect in which Hobbes's project differs from Leibniz's, and in this case from Descartes's too. Leibniz's conception of mathematics, like that of Descartes, is of a highly abstract symbolic algebra. Hobbes, on the contrary, conceives of arithmetic and geometry as the real sciences, whereas algebra is merely an art of discovery. He disparages analysis and praises synthesis in the *Elements* (EW i. 314–17) for almost exactly the same reasons that Descartes praises analysis and disparages synthesis. In his *Six Lessons to the Savilian Professors of Mathematics* he goes further, arguing that geometry is superior to arithmetic because it deals directly with sensible entities. Indeed, he goes so far as to deny Wallis's Euclidean definition of the line as 'length without breadth', maintaining that geometers deal with real sensible lines but ignore their breadth (EW vii. 202). This thoroughly empiricist approach to mathematics leads him to reject the use of symbols in anything other than invention: they are conventional and arbitrary, they prolong rather than shorten mathematical demonstrations, and they are of no value in the communication of results, where they must be translated into the things they represent (EW vii. 248 ff.). So the model of mathematical reasoning for Hobbes is not algebra, which is just arbitrary notation, but geometry, where one deals directly with the sensible objects under investigation: lines, angles, curves, and so on.[15]

Hobbes's computational conception of reasoning is something which complements his mechanistic conception of nature, but it does not derive from his mechanism. Both his general conception and his terminology are strongly reminiscent of Ramus' 'Lectures on Dialectic', which appeared in his *Scholae in liberales artes* of 1569. For Ramus, analysis is construed primarily in didactic terms, as a way of taking apart some illustrative or exemplary text, and synthesis, which he calls *genesis* or *compositio*, is the reassembly of the elements thus arrived at by the pupil in an instructive way. As Ong has pointed out, such genesis or composition 'is not a birth or genesis so much as an assembly-line performance'.[16] It bears the traces of the mechanical mnemonic procedures that it replaces. Leibniz is not unaware of his indebtedness to Ramus (see, for example, GP vii. 516 ff.), but he is doing much more than simply refurbishing old rules of reasoning, whether Ramist or of any other variety. That he is concerned with rules is clear: as he writes in his Preface to Nizolius' *On The True Principles of Philosophy*, 'it is the proper task of the logician to teach the rules by which truth is to be achieved and confirmed, as well as all the devices for invention and judgment' (GP iv. 150). But 'Leibniz's rules are modelled on algebra—or, more precisely, on the 'General Characteristic' which algebra ultimately derives its rules from— and this means that their function is different from that envisaged by Ramus, or Hobbes, or Descartes. It is no longer a question of communicating already defined and classified ideas, but of formulating rules which govern the operations of thought and language.

---

[15] See Leibniz's reply to Hobbes in his 'Dialogue on the Connection between Words and Things' (GP vii. 190–3). Hobbes inaugurated a strong empiricist tradition of thinking about mathematics in England in the 17th and early 18th cents.; for details cf. H. M. Pycior, 'Mathematics and Philosophy: Wallis, Hobbes, Barrow, and Berkeley', *Journal of the History of Ideas*, 48 (1987), 265–86.

[16] W. Ong, *Ramus, Method, and the Decay of Dialogue* (Cambridge, Mass., 1958), 264. On Hobbes's familiarity with Ramus's work, cf. Ong, 'Hobbes and Talon's Ramist Rhetoric in English', *Transactions of the Cambridge Bibliographical Society*, 1 (1951), 260–9.

Leibniz's conception of a 'philosophical language' is not one of a language merely organizing words with completely independent meanings: the algebraic rules impose their own structure on the language, just as they imposed their own structure on mathematics in Descartes's *Geometry*.

Leibniz's computational conception of inference is quite different from Ramist and late scholastic conceptions of rules of reasoning, and we cannot simply translate Descartes's criticisms of the latter into criticisms of the former. I said at the end of the last chapter that Descartes attempts to understand proof in terms of an instantaneous grasp, so that we can move from premisses to conclusion in the one step, whereas Leibniz gets rid of the need to think through each step in a proof by making our traversal of these steps not instantaneous but mechanical, something which does not require us to stop and reflect at each step, yet which compels intellectual assent. There are, of course, some very questionable aspects of Leibniz's overall conception. He models all reasoning on this a priori, deductive, and mechanical prototype. But his idea that all truths have an a priori proof—that 'all things are understood by God a priori, as eternal truths; for He does not need experience, and yet all things are known by Him adequately' (GP vii. 296)—caused him immense problems, and indeed verges on unintelligibility.[17] Moreover, his general idea that discovery of the right premisses and symbolism would put an end to any dispute is implausibly naïve, even if we accept that his famous statement that any dispute can be resolved by the disputants saying to one another 'Let us calculate!' and 'by taking to pen and ink, we should soon settle the question' (GP vii. 200–1; C p. 156) is to be understood as a calculation of probability rather than truth.[18] Let us abstract from these difficulties, however, and consider the merits of Leibniz's account simply as an account of deductive inference. How does Descartes's account compare with it?

There are two elements in Descartes's account that must be

---

[17] See I. Hacking, 'A Leibnizian Theory of Truth', in M. Hooker (ed.), *Leibniz* (Manchester, 1982), 185–95.
[18] See I. Hacking, *The Emergence of Probability* (Cambridge, 1975), 135.

kept distinct here. The first is a theory about what process we engage in when we move from the premisses of an argument to its conclusion, and in particular what is essential in this process and what is redundant in it. The second is a theory about the justification of inference. For Descartes, the connection between premisses and conclusion is established when we grasp that connection in an unmediated way, and this grasp also shows us that the inference is a legitimate one. Descartes and Leibniz clearly differ on the first question. On Descartes's account, any intermediate steps linking premisses and conclusion, which may need to be introduced if we do not grasp the connection immediately, have to be jettisoned (or, more strictly speaking, run together) for us to be able to grasp the connection in an *intuitus*, and it is only when we have grasped the connection in this way that we have grasped it clearly and distinctly. For Leibniz, on the other hand, the intermediate steps are constitutive of the connection between premisses and conclusion. They tell one what this connection is by indicating what the route from the one to the other is. This is especially important for Leibniz in a way that it is not for Descartes. In the letter to Gabriel Wagner he writes:

Everything discovered by the understanding has been discovered by good rules of logic, although these rules may not have been made explicit or noted down at the beginning ... There is no doubt that someone skilled in the art of reasoning proceeds with more acuteness than others. (GP vii. 523.)

In other words, the rules of deduction constitute a method of discovery for Leibniz. This makes them extremely important: we cannot develop a *method* of discovery if we simply discard rules of inference once they have served their purpose in some particular demonstration. The fact that Leibniz construes deduction as a method of discovery shapes the way in which he conceives of the deductive process. Descartes, on the other hand, considers that deduction is incapable of yielding new truths, and consequently deductive steps, and the rules that govern them, are of no interest to him.

On the second question, Descartes's view is that by compacting inferential steps until we come to a direct connection between premisses and conclusion we put ourselves in a position where we are able to have a clear and distinct idea of the connection, and this provides us with a guarantee of certainty. No further justification is needed. I have already indicated some of the problems with this approach, in particular the assumption that because no further justification is needed, no further elucidation is needed. Descartes makes this assumption in the case of truth, as we saw in the last chapter, and Locke makes the closely connected assumption (which seems to me very much in the spirit of Descartes's thought) that a self-evident truth is an independent truth, as we have just seen. Leibniz is surely on much firmer ground here. He is able to provide an elucidation of inferential procedures in a way that Descartes cannot, and the most elementary elucidation must surely lead one to doubt that compacting inferential steps in the way envisaged by Descartes brings one to a direct connection between premisses and conclusion: rather, it would remove any such connections, direct or otherwise.

APPENDIX

The Terms 'a Priori' and 'a Posteriori' in the *Reply to the Second Set of Objections to the Meditations*

At the beginning of the *Reply to the Second Set of Objections*, Descartes associates the terms 'analysis' and 'synthesis' with more traditional sets of dichotomous terms. In the Latin text, we are told:

Demonstrandi autem ratio duplex est, alia scilicet per analysim, alia per synthesim. Analysis veram viam ostendit per quam res methodice & tanquam a priori inventa est . . . Synthesis è contra per viam oppositam & tanquam a posteriori quaesitam (etsi saepe ipsa probatio sit in hac magis a priori quàm in illâ) . . . (AT vii. 155–6.)

Further, the method of demonstration is twofold, involving analysis and synthesis. Analysis shows the true way by which a thing has been discovered methodically and as it were *a priori* . . . Synthesis on the other hand takes the opposite path, one which is as it were *a posteriori* (even though the demonstration itself is often, in synthesis, more *a priori* than in analysis).

This is indeed puzzling: analysis is 'as it were *a priori*', synthesis is 'as it were *a posteriori*', but synthesis is usually more a priori than analysis! In his edition of Descartes's philosophical writings, Alquié has pointed out (ii. 583 n. 1) that this Latin text makes more sense if we take the terms a priori and a posteriori, as they figure outside the parentheses, in a broad and non-technical sense. What the passage then says is simply that analysis comes first, that is, we do analysis first, and synthesis comes afterwards, that is, we do the synthesis after we have done the analysis. But, as he points out, the trouble is that this does not square with the French version, prepared by Clerselier and, we have every reason to believe, checked and authorized by Descartes himself. The passage in the French version runs:

La maniere de démontrer est double: l'vne se fait par l'analyse ou resolution, & l'autre par la synthese ou composition. L'analyse montre la vray voye par laquelle vne chose a esté methodiquement inuentée, & fait voir comment les effets dependent des choses ... La synthese, au contraire, par vne voye tout autre, & comme en examinant les causes par leurs effets (bien que la preuue qu'elle contient soit souuent aussi des effets par les causes) ... (AT ix$_i$. 121–2.)

Further, the method of demonstration is twofold, involving analysis or resolution and synthesis or composition. Analysis shows the true way by which a thing has been discovered methodically, and shows us how the effects depend on the causes ... Synthesis on the other hand takes the opposite path, and examines as it were the causes through the effects (even though often effects are also demonstrated here through their causes).

Alquié maintains that this version renders the passage incomprehensible. Clerselier, he tells us, is taking a priori reasoning in the medieval sense of reasoning that proceeds from cause to effect, or from principle to consequence, and a posteriori reasoning as reasoning that proceeds from effect to cause, or consequence to principle. But analysis proceeds from effect to cause, or consequence to principle, so it should be a posteriori, not 'as it were a priori'. Conversely with synthesis. But how, Alquié asks, could Clerselier have made such an obvious error, and how could Descartes have missed it? In short, the problem we are faced with is that the Latin text is hard to make sense of as it stands, but the only gloss that seems to give it some sense conflicts with the gloss provided in the authorized translation, a gloss which seems to make the text even more obscure.

The situation is, however, not as dire as Alquié would have us believe. His reading of the relation between causes and effects in the Clerselier version surely gets it the wrong way round. In saying that analysis shows us how effects depend upon their causes, Descartes/Clerselier is not saying that we start from causes and determine their effects, but rather that we start with effects and show what the causes that they depend upon are. Similarly, in saying that synthesis examines causes through their effects he is not saying that we start from effects and infer causes, but that we start with causes and determine their truth, generality, and so on by looking at their effects. This reading is just as natural as Alquié's, and it is inconceivable that Clerselier/Descartes would have got analysis and synthesis the wrong way round. Not only was it a point central to discussion of method from the mid-sixteenth century onwards, but the construal of analysis and synthesis in terms of 'resolution' and 'composition', which are explicitly and undeniably procedures that proceed from effect to cause and cause to effect respectively, shows beyond doubt what Clerselier/Descartes had in mind. Moreover, we can now make sense of the phrase in parentheses: synthesis proceeds from postulated principles or effects, but this will usually involve demonstrating the consequences or effects from the principles or causes. The problem is that while the French version now makes sense in its own right it no longer looks like a translation of the Latin. Analysis is not a priori in the usual sense, nor synthesis a posteriori.

In response to this, one thing we could do would be to follow Alquié and take the terms very generally. But this requires us to take the 'a priori' in the main text in a very general sense and the 'a priori' in parentheses in a reasonably strict technical sense. This is somewhat gratuitous. Moreover, if Alquié were right in his general construal of the terms, the *tanquam*—'as it were'—would be wholly mysterious. It is not that analysis 'as it were' comes first, it very obviously and literally comes first. I do not have a completely satisfactory solution to this problem, but I suggest the following, which is at least more plausible than Alquié's reading. The terms 'a priori' and 'a posteriori' have a reasonably clear meaning for us, one we owe to Kant, although Leibniz may have been largely responsible for the modern distinction. Earlier usages are much less clear, and what was a priori and a posteriori in scholastic philosophy depended upon whether one was considering the order of being or the order of knowing. The terms literally mean 'from what comes before' and 'from what comes after', and the scholastic usage depends on the Aristotelian doctrine of the distinction between what is prior in nature and what is prior in knowledge. Something is prior in nature (*priora natura*) to something else if it could not exist without it: in this sense causes are prior to their effects. But something is prior in knowledge (*priora nobis*) to something else if we could not know the latter without knowing the former: in this sense effects may be prior to their causes. Analysis may well be a priori in the order of knowing, and it is after all the order of knowing that is most relevant here. As regards synthesis, it is a posteriori in the order of knowing, although the form the synthetic demonstration takes may be that of deducing consequences or effects from principles or causes. The problem is compounded by the fact that it was usual in medieval discussions of these issues—which originated in the Galen-inspired *Prohemium* to Averroës' commentary on Aristotle's *Physics*—to consider that the orders of knowing and being coincided in the case of mathematics. In these circumstances, the terms a priori and a posteriori are relatively unhelpful in throwing light on the other distinctions, and resolution and composition would appear to serve us better in trying to determine what is involved in analysis and synthesis.

4

Scientific Reasoning

ARTICLE 64 of Part II of the *Principles of Philosophy* is entitled:

That I do not accept or desire in physics any principles other than those accepted in geometry or abstract mathematics; because all the phenomena of nature are explained thereby, and demonstrations concerning them which are certain can be given.

In elucidation, Descartes writes:

For I frankly admit that I know of no material substance other than that which is divisible, has shape, and can move in every possible way, and this the geometers call quantity and take as the object of their demonstrations. Moreover, our concern is exclusively with the division, shape and motions of this substance, and nothing concerning these can be accepted as true unless it be deduced (*deducatur*) from indubitably true common notions with such certainty that it can be regarded as a mathematical demonstration (*demonstratione*). And because all natural phenomena can be explained in this way, as one can judge from what follows, I believe that no other physical principles should be accepted or even desired. (AT viii₁. 78–9.)

This claim is at first surprising in the light of his attacks on traditional syllogistic and synthetic forms of demonstration, attacks which rule out deduction having any value. Moreover, it will be clear by now that scientific reasoning provides the context of assessment for conceptions of inference on Descartes's view—that is the whole point of pitting 'method' against syllogistic—so if his own conception, including his dismissal of deduction, does not stand up in this context it is in deep trouble.

Before we consider just how deep this trouble is, however, it is advisable that we are clear about what the word 'deduction' means in this context. We have already touched on this question, and noted that, for Descartes, it has a much broader meaning than that we now attribute to it. In particular, it does not necessarily indicate a consequential direction. Clarke has pointed out that deduction may amount to proof or explanation in Descartes. In the latter case the epistemic direction is the opposite of the consequential direction, in that we may be seeking to explain a conclusion we know to be true. This is an important feature of Descartes's account of deduction, as we shall see in the second section of this chapter. Clarke also points out that 'it is impossible to avoid the conclusion that Descartes uses the term "*déduire*" to mean a detailed enumeration of steps in an argument in such a way that the term no longer characterizes the logic of the argument but rather the step-by-step narration which is involved in its articulation.'[1] If this narrative sense of 'deduce' were the only one at issue in the *Principles* passage then it might appear that there is no problem of reconciliation, as Descartes has effectively committed himself to nothing in the passage. But I think it is clear that it is not. The 'deduction' is one from 'indubitably true' common notions and it is one which brings with it 'certainty'. Whether or not Descartes is interested in the logical features of such a deduction is a different question from whether he is describing something which has logical features, and here these logical features require us to take seriously his claim that deduction is to be used. We shall look at this question first.

THE METHOD OF DISCOVERY

We saw in the last chapter that Descartes not only associates synthesis with deduction, but also takes analysis in such a way that it comprises what Pappus called problematical analysis, excluding theoretical analysis: that is to say, he takes analysis to be a

---

[1] D. Clarke, *Descartes' Philosophy of Science* (Manchester, 1982), 209.

problem-solving procedure, not a procedure for finding theorems. The distinction between analysis and synthesis is, for Descartes, effectively the distinction between problem-solving and deduction, and in advocating analysis and disparaging synthesis he is, as we have seen, advocating problem-solving techniques and rejecting the attempt to advance knowledge deductively. Yet in the passage that I have just quoted from the *Principles* he appears to be advocating a deductive process based on demonstration from indubitable axioms. Moreover, as well as apparently advocating deduction, he on occasion appears to reject a problem-solving approach to natural philosophy. In a letter to Mersenne of 11 October 1638, for example, he writes that Galileo's *Two New Sciences* seems to him to be

very deficient, in that [Galileo] is continually digressing and does not stop to give a complete explanation of any matter. This shows that he has not examined things in order and that, without considering the first causes of nature, he has only sought to account for some particular effects, and thus that he has built without foundation. (AT ii. 380.)

Part of what Descartes objects to here is the fact that Galileo has only provided a kinematics of motion, but he is also questioning whether a physics not based upon first principles is at all worth while. Yet Galileo's procedure seems in many ways to parallel Descartes's own problem-solving approach in his *Geometry*.

One feature of Descartes's account that gives it an especially deductivist flavour is his attempt to reduce physical theory to applied mathematics. This is evident in his early call for a universal mathematics in Rule 4 of the *Regulae*:

... all and only those questions in which order and measure are investigated belong to mathematics, and it makes no difference whether one is concerned with measure in respect of numbers, shapes, stars, sounds or whatever other object. And consequently I saw that there must be some general science which explains everything that it is possible for one to seek concerning order and measure, these having no special subject matter. This science is 'universal mathematics'. (AT x. 377–8.)

There is some dispute as to the role that this universal mathematics plays in Descartes's later thought, and in particular its relation to his concept of 'method', but this need not detain us here,[2] for it is not in dispute that mathematics plays a fundamental role in his natural philosophy. The discussion of simple natures in the later Rule 12 of the *Regulae* indicates that the simple natures from which our reasoning must start are either mathematical (shape and extension) or kinematic (motion). But the most striking attempt to construe all of our knowledge in mathematical terms comes at the end of the *Meditations*. Descartes introduces there the distinction between the formal and objective reality of ideas. The formal reality of an idea is the reality which an idea has in virtue of its being a mode of a thinking substance. Its objective reality, on the other hand, depends upon what it is the idea of: it depends upon its object. Although in the *Meditations* Descartes moves from the objective reality of an idea to its extra-mental existence he does not move from *any* object of an idea to its extra-mental existence, nor, when he does make the move, is it made in the same way in each case: the move from my idea of God to his extra-mental existence, for example, is not made in the same way as the move from my ideas of sensible objects to their extra-mental existence. The principal function of the objective reality argument is to specify the candidates for existence and these candidates are often radically distinct from what we might judge on the basis of sense experience to exist.

The amount of objective reality an idea has depends upon the amount of formal reality its object would have if that object existed. In this sense, ideas represent possible objects which have varying degrees of formal reality. But do we know that all our ideas represent objects that are in fact possible? In answering this question in the *Reply to the First Set of Objections to the*

---

[2] Two of the best discussions of this issue are J.-L. Marion, *Sur l'ontologie grise de Descartes* (Paris, 1981) and J. Schuster, 'Descartes' *Mathesis Universalis*, 1619–28', in S. Gaukroger (ed.), *Descartes* (Sussex, 1980), 41–96. Marion argues that universal mathematics is a precursor to method, whereas Schuster argues that method replaces universal mathematics. Since nothing in my own argument here hinges on this question, I shall remain agnostic.

Meditations, Descartes invokes the doctrine of clear and distinct ideas, telling us that 'in the concept or idea of everything that is clearly and distinctly conceived, possible existence is contained'. Ideas which are not clear and distinct are rather more problematic:

We must observe that those ideas that do not contain a true and immutable nature, but only a fictitious one due to a mental synthesis, can be by that same mind analysed, not merely by abstraction but by a clear and distinct mental operation; hence it will be clear that those things which the understanding cannot analyse have not been put together by it. For example, when I think of a winged horse, or of a lion actually existing, or of a triangle inscribed in a square, I can easily understand that I can on the contrary think of a horse without wings, of a lion as not existing and of a triangle apart from a square, and so forth, and that hence these things have no true and immutable nature. But if I think of the triangle or the square (I pass by for the present the lion and the horse, because their natures are not wholly intelligible to us), then certainly whatever I recognise as being contained in the idea of the triangle, as that its angles are equal to two right angles, etc., I shall truly affirm of the triangle; and similarly, I shall truly affirm of the square whatsoever I find in the idea of it. For though I can think of the triangle, though stripping from it the equality of its angles to two right angles, yet I cannot deny that attribute of it by any clear and distinct mental operation, i.e. when I myself rightly understand what I say. (AT vii. 166.)

In other words, I can only be sure about—indeed, I can only really *ask* about—the objective reality of clear and distinct ideas, and it is objective reality that determines the possible existence of the object of the idea. The way in which Descartes sets up the argument makes it necessary that we first enquire about possible existence and his introduction of the doctrine of clear and distinct ideas seriously restricts the range of possible existents. Indeed, we seem to be left with exclusively mathematical entities. As he puts it in the *Sixth Meditation*:

We must allow that corporeal things exist. However, they are perhaps not exactly as we perceive them by the senses, for sense perception is very obscure and confused in many cases. But at least it can be allowed that everything that I conceive in them clearly and distinctly—i.e. everything, generally speaking, that can be conceived in purely mathematical terms [*quae in purae matheseos objecto comprehenduntur*]—is truly to be recognised as a material object. (AT vii. 80.)

On other occasions he goes further, maintaining that the realization of mathematical entities in the form of actually existing objects is nothing more or less than the corporeal world. This strategy is made clear in his answer to a question from Burman. He explains:

All mathematical demonstrations deal with true and real entities, and the entire subject matter of mathematics and everything it deals with is a true and real entity. The subject matter has a true and real nature, just as much as the subject matter of physics itself. The only difference is that physics considers its subject matter to comprise not just something which is true and real, but something which has an actual and particular existence. Mathematics, on the other hand, considers its subject matter as something merely possible, i.e. as something which does not exist in space but is capable of doing so. (AT v. 160.)

Descartes is concerned to give a mathematical account of physical phenomena and this is to be achieved, at least in part, by construing these phenomena in terms of extension, which renders them directly susceptible to geometrical treatment.[3] The 'simple natures' and 'first principles' that he refers to are graspable in terms of clear and distinct ideas because they are mathematical, and in virtue of this they are able to serve as a foundation for the rest of knowledge. But to say this is not to say that the rest of knowledge can be deduced from them. Descartes *seems* to be saying this in Article 64 of Part II of the *Principles*, but, almost immediately after, in Article 4 of Part III, entitled 'Of phenomena or experiments and of their use in philosophy', he writes:

The principles that we have already discovered are so numerous and fertile that much more follows from them than we find in this visible universe, and even more than we could ever examine in our minds. Let us now briefly describe the principal natural phenomena whose causes are to

---

[3] On this question generally see my 'Descartes' Project for a Mathematical Physics', in S. Gaukroger (ed.), *Descartes*, 97–140.

be investigated here, not so as to prove anything from them, since we wish to deduce effects from their causes rather than causes from their effects, but so that we can select for consideration some of the innumerable effects which we judge to be produced by those causes. (AT viii₁. 81.)

The problem with a purely deductive approach is, in short, that one is able to deduce too much. The first principles take us to every possible world, which is of no use since this would be unmanageable, and perhaps even incomprehensible to us, and in any case all we want is an account of the actual world. It is at this point, according to the Article's title, that experiment comes in. The point is elaborated upon in the sixth part of the *Discourse on Method*, and this important passage is worth quoting in full:

The order which I have followed [in the *Dioptrics* and the *Meteorology*] is as follows. First, I have attempted generally to discover the principles or first causes of everything which is or could be in the world, without in this connection considering anything but God alone, who has created the world, and without drawing them from any source except certain seeds of truth which are naturally in our minds. Next I considered what were the first and most common effects that could be deduced from these causes, and it seems to me that in this way I found the heavens, the stars, an earth, and even on the earth, water, air, fire, the minerals and a few other such things which are the most common and simple of any that exist, and consequently the easiest to understand. Then, when I wished to descend to those that were more particular, there were so many objects of various kinds that I did not believe it possible for the human mind to distinguish the forms or species of body which are on the earth from the infinity of others which might have been, had it been the will of God to put them there, or consequently to make them of use to us, if it were not that one arrives at the causes through the effects and avails oneself of many specific experiments. In subsequently passing over in my mind all the objects which have been presented to my senses, I dare to say that I have not noticed anything that I could not easily explain in terms of the principles that I have discovered. But I must also admit that the power of nature is so great and extensive, and these principles so simple and general, that I hardly observed any effect that I did not immediately realize could be deduced from the principles in many different ways. The greatest difficulty is usually to discover in which of these ways the effect depends on them. In this situation, so far as I know the only thing that can be done is to try and find experiments which are such that their result varies depending upon which of them provides the correct explanation. (AT vi. 63–5.)

If we think of first principles as providing a context for explanations, we can reconcile Descartes's reliance on first principles with his general advocacy of problem-solving, as opposed to theorem-finding. The first principles do genuinely provide foundations for knowledge, and our results have to be derivable from them if we are to be certain that they constitute knowledge. But this does not mean that we actually arrive at those results by deriving them from first principles. What it means is that the results must be compatible with the first principles. The procedure by which we actually arrive at the results occurs at a completely different level. In a letter to Vatier of 22 February 1638, Descartes, in reply to queries about the *Discourse*, says that although he was not able to use his method there, he has provided a sample of it in his discussion of the rainbow, in the *Meteorology* (AT i. 559). And in the *Meteorology* itself he tells us that his account of the rainbow is the most appropriate example 'to show how, by means of the method which I use, one can attain knowledge which was not available to those whose writings we possess' (AT vi. 325).

As in the *Geometry*, Descartes presents a problem which earlier writers had been unable to solve (he did not know of Kepler's work on the rainbow), and he uses the solution of the problem as an exemplification of his method. That is to say, we start from a problem to be solved, not from first principles. The problem to be solved is that of explaining the angle at which the bows of the rainbow appear in the sky. He begins by noting that rainbows are not only formed in the sky, but also in fountains and showers in the presence of sunlight. This leads him to formulate the hypothesis that the phenomenon is caused by light reacting on drops of water. To test this hypothesis, he constructs a glass model of the raindrop, comprising a large glass sphere filled with water, and, standing with his back to the sun, he holds up the sphere in the sun's light, moving it up and down so that colours are produced. Then, if we let the light from the sun come

from the part of the sky marked AFZ, and my eye be at point E, then when I put this globe at the place BCD, the part of it at D seems to me wholly red and incomparably more brilliant than the rest. And whether I move towards it or step back from it, or move it to the right or the left, or even turn it in a circle around my head, then provided the line DE always makes an angle of around 42° with the line EM, which one must imagine to extend from the centre of the eye to the centre of the sun, D always appears equally red. But as soon as I made this angle DEM the slightest bit larger, the redness disappeared. And when I made it a little bit smaller it did not disappear completely in the one stroke but first divided as into

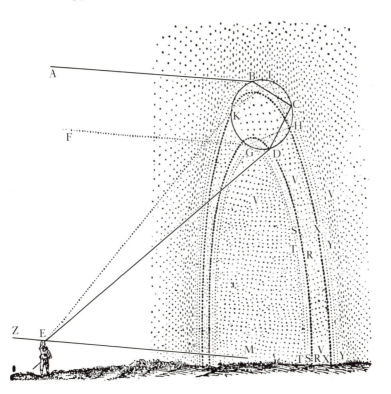

two less brilliant parts in which could be seen yellow, blue, and other colours. Then, looking towards the place marked K on the globe, I perceived that, making the angle KEM around 52°, K also seemed to be coloured red, but not so brilliant as D ... (AT vi. 326–7.)

Descartes then describes how he covered the globe at all points except B and D. The ray still emerged, showing that the primary and secondary bows are caused by two refractions and one or two internal reflections of the incident ray. He next describes how the same effect can be produced with a prism, and this indicates that neither a curved surface nor reflection are necessary for colour dispersion. Moreover, the prism experiment shows that the effect does not depend on the angle of incidence and that one refraction is sufficient for its production. Finally, Descartes calculates from the refractive index of rainwater what an observer would see when light strikes a drop of water at varying angles of incidence, and finds that the optimum difference for visibility between incident and refracted rays is for the former to be viewed at an angle of 41° to 42° and the latter at an angle of 51° to 52° (AT vi. 336), which is exactly what the hypothesis predicts.

Another example of analysis is Descartes's account of how he discovered the sine law of refraction in the second Discourse of the *Dioptrics*.[4] He begins by constructing a model for the refraction of light which consists in a tennis ball which strikes a frail canvas, penetrating it and as a result losing half its initial speed. Abstracting from extraneous features of the ball, such as its weight and size, the force of motion of the ball can then be determined:

In order to know what path the ball will follow, let us observe again that its motion is entirely different from its determination to move in one direction rather than another, from which it follows that their quantities must be examined separately. And let us also note that, of the two parts which we can imagine this determination to be composed of, only the one that was making the ball tend in a downwards direction can be changed by the encounter with the canvas in any way, while the one that was

---

[4] I am concerned here with Descartes's account of how he discovered the sine law, not with how he actually discovered it. On this latter question see ch. 4 of J. Schuster, 'Descartes and the Scientific Revolution' (Ph.D. thesis, Princeton University, 1977).

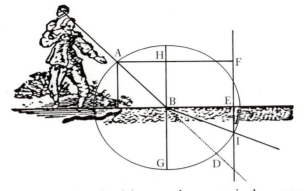

making the ball tend to the right must always remain the same as it was, because the canvas is not in any way opposed to it in this direction. Then, having described the circle AFD with B as its centre, and drawn the three straight lines AC, HB, FE at right angles with CBE, such that the distance between FE and HB is twice that between HB and AC, we shall see that the ball must tend towards the point I. For, since the ball loses half its speed in going through the canvas CBE, it must employ twice the time it took above the canvas from A to B to travel below from any point on the circumference of the circle AFD. And since it loses nothing whatsoever of its former determination to advance to the right, in twice the time it took to pass from the line AC to HB it must cover twice the distance in the same direction, and consequently it must arrive at the same point on the straight line FE simultaneously with its reaching a point on the circumference of the circle ADF. But this would be impossible if it did not proceed towards I, as this is the only point below the canvas CBE where the circle AFD and the straight line EF intersect. (AT vi. 97–8.)

Descartes then considers cases where the ball, for example on striking water, is reflected or where its speed changes at the point of refraction. He is then able to move from the model to light itself:

Finally, insofar as the action of light follows the same laws as the movement of the ball in this respect, one must say that, when its rays pass obliquely from one transparent body to another which receives them more or less easily than the first, they are deflected in such a way that they are always inclined on the surfaces of these bodies on the side of the body which receives them more easily than they are on the other side; and this occurs exactly in proportion as one receives it more easily than the other. (AT vi. 100.)

The geometry of the situation is then straightforward. If we let V_{AB} be the speed of the incident ray and V_{BI} be the speed of the

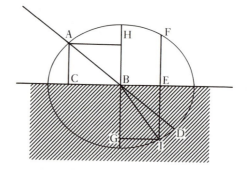

refracted ray, then $V_{AB} = kV_{BI}$ (where k equals one-half in Descartes's example). And since the horizontal speed is not affected by the impact, then $V_{AB}\sin \angle ABH = V_{BI}\sin \angle BIE$. Consequently, the ratio between $\sin \angle ABH$ and $\sin \angle BIE$ is k, where the value of k for different combinations of media is something to be determined experimentally (AT vi. 102). This completes the analytic solution to the problem. The synthetic solution would simply rearrange the steps so that a presentation from first principles could be given.

The approach, as Descartes outlines it, in the case of the discovery of the sine law, the calculation of the angles of the bows of a rainbow, and the solution of Pappus' locus-problem, is the same, and in each case it consists purely in analysis. In each case we take a specific problem bequeathed by antiquity and solve it using procedures compatible with the basic precepts of Cartesian science. We then try to incorporate the solution within a general system which has as its foundations those truths which we cannot doubt because we have a clear and distinct grasp of them (and because God guarantees those truths of which we have such a grasp). Once we understand this procedure—discovery by problem-solving and then incorporation of the result into a general system with indubitable foundations—we can begin to understand a little better the nature of Descartes's objection to what he takes to be Galileo's approach. Descartes, as we have seen, complains that Galileo is concerned simply with particular effects, and consequently 'builds without foundation'. The point is made again in connection with Galileo's account of the principle of the lever, which, we are told, only explains *how* and not *why* (AT ii. 433). As I have indicated, part of what is at issue here is Galileo's failure to provide a dynamics, but just as important is his failure to incorporate his account into a comprehensive natural philosophy. Such an incorporation provides a foundation for one's explanations of particular natural phenomena. What use one is able to make of this foundation will vary considerably, however, depending on how successfully one can connect one's accounts of particular phenomena to the foundational principles. In the case of Descartes's account of the angles at which the bows of the rainbow appear in the sky, the hypothesis that is introduced is verified and other possible explanations are excluded to such an extent that he effectively presents us with a crucial experiment. A reasonably direct connection between the explanation, the crucial theoretical element in which is his use of the sine law, and basic mathematical and natural philosophical principles can be established here. But such paradigm cases are rare, and in the usual case—for instance virtually all of Parts III and IV of the *Principles*—we are left with hypotheses not capable of conclusive verification, and here no direct connection with first principles is forthcoming. Of course, Descartes treats this as a temporary situation and hopes that such hypotheses will ultimately be verified or dispensed with, but this is to be achieved not by exploring their connections with first principles, and more specifically not by trying to develop some logical apparatus by which they can be derived from first principles, but by experiment.

In sum, Descartes's procedure in natural philosophy does begin with problem-solving, and his 'method' is designed to facilitate such problem-solving. The problems have to be posed in quantitative terms and there are a number of constraints on what form an acceptable solution takes: one cannot posit 'occult qualities', one must seek 'simple natures', and so on. The solution is then tested experimentally to determine how well it holds up compared with other possible explanations meeting the same constraints which also appear to account for the facts. Finally, the solution must be incorporated into Descartes's system of natural philosophy, a system which it is the principal aim of the *Principles* to set out in detail. This system has a number of advantages over other prevailing corpuscular-mechanical philosophies: it is much more systematic and quantitative than they,[5] as well as having a novel and deep foundation. The successful incorporation of experimentally verified results into this system is what constitutes indubitable knowledge, that is, absolute certainty, and at the end of the *Principles* Descartes indicates that he believes he has achieved this in mathematics, in his account of the transmission of light, and in a few other selected areas.

THE EPISTEMIC VALUE OF DEDUCTION

As we saw in the last chapter, a number of Descartes's criticisms of traditional syllogistic—and, by extension, deductive reasoning generally—turn on the argument that it cannot yield new truths. The apparently deductive structure of the *Principles*, I have just argued, is not actually in conflict with this since what the *Principles* provide is not a means of producing new truths but rather a systematic natural philosophy into which our physical results, arrived at by hypothetical and experimental means, must be incorporated. Through such an incorporation, those few propositions which we can grasp clearly and distinctly can be related directly to the foundational principles, whereas those that cannot be grasped can at least be allocated a (perhaps provisional) place within the whole structure.

---

[5] On this question see R. Lenoble, *Mersenne ou la naissance de mécanisme* (Paris, 1971).

The difference between Descartes and Leibniz here is worth spelling out. For Descartes, part of the inappropriateness of a purely deductive system of natural philosophy derives from the fact that the first principles are such that much more follows from them than occurs in the actual world.[6] If we were simply to start from first principles and systematically to attempt to extend our knowledge deductively, we would very quickly become swamped by a myriad of possibilities, and we would be unable to distinguish by these means what pertains to the actual world and what does not. Leibniz would have had no serious quarrel with this. As we saw in the last chapter, in the letter to Wagner of 1696 he makes it clear that deductive processes are only really of use once one already has a reasonable store of information. Indeed, the procedure Leibniz recommends, that of starting with a comprehensive amount of information, using the deductive system to survey and impose an order on it, and then, using the order discerned, going on to new discoveries by deductive means, is, at least in broad outline, not too dissimilar to Descartes's procedure in all but the last respect. But the two approaches do differ very radically in the last respect, since Leibniz is maintaining that deduction by itself will yield new natural-philosophical truths whereas Descartes is denying this. What is fundamentally at issue here is whether deduction can be epistemically informative.

Before we look at this question, a word of caution is necessary. It is important that we distinguish here between the justification of deduction in the context of scientific discovery and the justification of deduction *per se*. The former turns on questions of epistemic informativeness, the latter does not. That the latter does not is clear from the fact that $<P,P>$ is as good a deduction as any other, in logical terms. Deductive logic is designed to capture

[6] This is an especially serious problem for Descartes, since the only non-empirical constraint is what lies in God's power, and this is effectively no constraint at all. Some of the difficulties this raises are set out in a letter to Chanut of 6 June 1647: not only may there be other solar systems, etc. in a universe which, he argues, must be indefinitely large, but there may be other 'intelligent creatures in the stars or elsewhere' (AT v. 55). Such questions he prefers to leave open as we have no grounds for dealing with them, and they are certainly not the concern of the *Principles*.

systematic sets of relations between truths and to bring to light the characteristic features of these relations: in the course of this, philosophical or foundational questions may be raised, about the point of capturing truth-preserving rather than other semantic relationships, about how one explains what truth-preservation consists in, and so on. Questions of justification may also be raised, but these are quite different questions from those we are currently concerned with and do not turn on questions of epistemic informativeness. Our aim in justifying deduction, as Dummett rightly argues, 'is not to persuade anyone, not even ourselves, to employ deductive arguments: it is to find a satisfactory explanation of the role of such arguments in our use of language'.[7] Descartes would completely disagree with this assessment, and, as we saw in Chapter 2, would argue that such basic inferential moves are beyond analysis, explanation, and justification: they are simply primitive and we know them by the natural light of reason. This is not the issue that we are currently concerned with. Our current concern is with the role of formalized deductive arguments, especially syllogistic arguments, in the discovery of new results in natural philosophy. I am not saying that questions of the justification of deduction were always clearly separated from questions of the role of deduction in scientific inference, for they were not—it was a prevalent assumption in the seventeenth century that syllogistic, in both its logical and heuristic aspects, could be justified if and only if it could show its epistemic worth—but the basis for a distinction was there, and while the questions are related in Descartes, we can find sets of considerations much more relevant to the one than to the other. Let us look, then, at the question of epistemic informativeness.

At first sight, it seems uncontentious to say that some deductions are epistemically informative and some are not, that is, that some lead us to new beliefs whereas others do not. It is hard to imagine how any argument of the form $<\{P \supset Q, P\}Q>$ could be epistemically informative for example, still less one of the form

[7] M. Dummett, 'The Justification of Deduction' (*Truth and Other Enigmas*, London, 1978), 296.

< P,P >. Yet both are formally valid deductions. On the other hand, it seems that some deductive arguments do make an epistemic advance. Consider the famous account of Aubrey, in his *Brief Lives*, of Hobbes's first encounter with Euclid's *Elements*:

> Being in a Gentelman's Library, Euclid's Elements lay open, and 'twas the 47 El. libri I. He read the Proposition. By G__, sayd he (he would now and then sweare an emphatical oath by way of emphasis), this is impossible! So he reads the Demonstration of it, which referred him back to another, which he also read. *Et sic deinceps* [and so on] that at last he was demonstratively convinced of that trueth. This made him in love with Geometry.

This is surely as clear a case as one could wish for of epistemic advance. Hobbes begins by believing something impossible but a deductive proof convinces him of its truth.

But if some deductions are epistemically informative and others are not, does this mean that epistemic advance is merely an accidental feature of some deductive arguments, and if so that there is nothing intrinsically epistemically informative about deduction? And if this is the case, what exactly does one learn from a deduction? I shall look at four kinds of response to the problem. They are: (1) to argue that all deductions are epistemically informative; (2) to argue that no deductions are epistemically informative; (3) to argue that epistemic informativeness derives from some intrinsic but non-logical feature of the deduction; (4) to argue that epistemic informativeness derives from a combination of intrinsic and extrinsic factors, in such a way that we can never guarantee epistemic informativeness. My overall aim is to show that, while Descartes defends (2), a good deal of what he needs is actually defensible on the basis of (4), and (4) is in fact the correct response.

1. Two defences of the view that all deductions are epistemically informative can be distinguished. The first trades on the fact that what appears in the conclusion of a deductive argument is a different statement from the statements making up the premisses, at least in all but the < P,P > case, which can be conceded as

uninformative. If we believe that $\ulcorner P \supset Q \urcorner$ and that P, for example, then *modus ponens* commits us to the belief that Q. Q is not one of the premisses, so we end up with a new belief as a result of the deduction. But what is at issue here is something so weak that it could be accepted by someone who believed that the conclusion was always contained in the premisses of deductive arguments. Just because we have a statement as the conclusion that does not appear in the premisses tells us nothing about whether a belief that the premisses are true is presupposed by, or is the same thing as, a belief that the conclusion is true, for example, and this is exactly the kind of thing that is at issue. If we construe epistemic informativeness too weakly we make it trivially true that deductions are epistemically informative but at the price of failing to capture what is at issue.

A second kind of defence of this view is to maintain that every deduction must make an epistemic advance because proof and epistemic advance are the same thing or aspects of the same thing. We noted one version of this kind of claim in the last chapter, when we looked at Leibniz's proof of $2 + 2 = 4$. The claim was that, since $2 + 2 = 4$ could be proved, as the conclusion of a deductive argument, from premisses including $1 + 1 = 2$, it is thereby shown that $1 + 1 = 2$ is more evident than $2 + 2 = 4$. But this is mistaken, as I argued. What the proof shows is that the truth of $2 + 2 = 4$ depends upon the truth of $1 + 1 = 2$, but not that its self-evidence does. $2 + 2 = 4$ is completely self-evident independently of its proof; the proof does *not* show us that it was not self-evident after all. Consequential and epistemic steps are different kinds of things.

2. Three versions of the view that no deductions are epistemically informative can be distinguished. The first is easily disposed of. We have seen that it solves nothing to weaken the notion of epistemic informativeness; it solves nothing to strengthen it either. Many critics of logic in antiquity and indeed up to the nineteenth century criticized syllogistic arguments for failing to yield anything new, where what is meant by 'new' effectively amounts to 'logically independent of the premisses'. This is part of many (but

not all) demands that the syllogism yield something factually new, and I believe it comes about largely, as I indicated in Chapter 1, from a conflation of sceptical arguments about the possibility of proof with arguments questioning the independence of the conclusion in inductive inferences. But whatever its source—and this is a case where the error is much easier to identify than its sources—it results in the absurd demand that the conclusion of a deductive argument should be logically independent of its premisses.

A second version of (2) is one which relies on the idea that the conclusion of a deductive argument is already contained in its premisses, so that in knowing the premisses one knows the conclusion. Consequently, what the deduction does is simply to make explicit something one already implicitly knows. No epistemic advance is possible in deduction, on this conception. This is a view that has been held in a number of versions: Plato held a very distinctive version of it in the context of a general theory of knowledge as recollection in the *Meno*; Descartes holds it, as we have seen; Mill held it in the form of the doctrine that the conclusion contains the same 'assertion' as the premisses in a deductive argument; and the logical positivists have held that logical and mathematical truths are analytic and consequently that we cannot actually learn anything new in deduction. The most striking problem with this approach is its sheer implausibility. Take the Hobbes case: can it really be maintained that Hobbes implicitly knew the theorem all along (since he knew the axioms from which it is deducible) or that he has learned nothing in deducing it, when he begins by conceiving it to be impossible before he has gone through the proof? Is the case where he begins by believing that colour dispersion cannot occur with a plane surface, and ends up being convinced experimentally that it can, *so* different from that in which he begins by thinking it impossible that, in right-angled triangles, the square on the side subtending the right angle is equal to the squares on the sides containing the right angle, and ends up being convinced by a deduction that it can? Everything about the phenomenology of the situation indicates that the two cases are identical at the level of epistemic advance. And if there is no relevant difference between the two and one still wishes to maintain that there can be no epistemic advance in deduction, then it would seem that one must bite the bullet and adopt the Platonic view, either in its original version, or in terms of some doctrine of innate ideas, or whatever. But then the argument is that there is no such thing as epistemic advance, and this is quite a different doctrine from that we are currently interested in.

A third version of (2) is advocated by Descartes. It consists in the idea that the deduction of results does not genuinely produce those results: deduction is a mode of presentation of results which have already been reached by analytic, problem-solving means. This doctrine was our concern in the last chapter, but aside from problems peculiar to the doctrine, which were covered there, there is again the general problem of plausibility. One could agree with Descartes that the deductive procedures he terms 'synthesis' may not always be the best way of coming by results in mathematics (something which even Leibniz accepted), but that they can never play this role is simply contrary to our experience: as the plausibility of the Hobbes case shows.

3. If we accept that deductions may sometimes be epistemically informative and sometimes not, how do we account for this difference? There is surely no *logical* feature of a deduction that results in epistemic informativeness, and the form of a deduction seems to bear no relation to its epistemic informativeness. 'Lewis Carroll arguments' are a good example here. In an argument such as:

No-one who is going to a party ever fails to brush his hair. No-one looks fascinating if he is untidy. Opium eaters have no self command. Everyone who has brushed his hair looks fascinating. No-one ever wears white kid gloves unless he is going to a party. A man is always untidy if he has no self-command. *Therefore*, opium eaters never wear white kid gloves.

it is the number of premises and their ingenious arrangement that prevents one from seeing whether the conclusion follows without setting out a reasonably formal derivation. But there is nothing at all special in this derivation about the way in which the conclusion is yielded.

The logicians of antiquity, realizing that epistemic informativeness could not be captured logically, attempted to capture the source of epistemic informativeness in non-logical terms. We looked at the attempts of Aristotle and the Stoics to do this in the first chapter. Aristotle's difficulty was that demonstrative syllogisms, supposedly the bearers of a special kind of epistemic informativeness (remembering that epistemic and consequential directions run counter to one another in demonstrative syllogisms), turn out to be indistinguishable from non-demonstrative syllogisms because Aristotle cannot provide any coherent account of what the difference lies in. In the case of the Stoics, the problem lies in the claim that the conditional premiss of 'scientific' demonstrations is rationally self-evident whereas the conclusion is non-evident, for on the face of it their degree of evidence is the same.

4. Whether a general account of the non-logical factors which contribute to epistemic informativeness can be provided, I leave open. It is clear, however, that an account that restricts itself to intrinsic factors, as the Aristotelian and Stoic accounts do, is not going to be successful. Whether a deduction is epistemically informative will depend to a large degree on extrinsic factors, such as our initial state of knowledge and our initial beliefs. After all, if the theorem that so surprised Hobbes had been familiar to him already, say through some practical knowledge in architecture or perspective, then the very same deduction would not have had the epistemic value that it did (although it might have had a different kind of epistemic value in that Hobbes would have learned that something he already knew could be derived from something else he knew, which he had not realized before). But nor is it wholly a question of extrinsic factors, for a deduction of the form $<P,P>$ will never have epistemic value, whereas even a simple one of the form $<\{\ulcorner P \supset Q \urcorner, \neg Q\}, \neg P>$ may have. Epistemic value is, then, neither wholly intrinsic nor extrinsic to deduction and, so far as we can tell, there is no way of guaranteeing in advance that our

deduction will be epistemically informative, contrary to the aspirations of ancient logicians.

Descartes rejects the view that deduction can be made epistemically informative, and he therefore rejects Aristotle's account. Two different issues must be kept distinct here, however: what Aristotle's account actually is and what Descartes takes it to be. These, as we have seen, are quite different from one another. Aristotle's account was taken to be an account of how novel scientific results can be yielded from epistemically informative demonstrative syllogisms, or chains of such syllogisms. It was taken that, in such syllogisms, the consequential direction and the purported epistemic direction coincided. Descartes rightly rejects the doctrine of the demonstrative syllogism, so interpreted, but his rejection goes too far, for it takes the form of an argument that no deduction can have epistemic value, at least where epistemic and consequential directions are supposed to coincide. This is not necessary for a defence of the role of experiment in scientific discovery, or for a defence of non-axiomatic problem-solving approaches: Leibniz manages to provide a conception of discovery which combines these with a commitment to the use of deduction in expanding and refining our knowledge, once experimental and problem-solving procedures have provided a substantial initial body of information. In rejecting a completely deductive approach to scientific discovery, Descartes opts for a completely non-deductive one, but it is simply unnecessary to go this far, and all one ends up with is a wholly implausible account which denies any epistemic value to the deduction of an apparently unknown conclusion from known premisses under any circumstances.

When we consider Aristotle's actual account, a number of similarities with Descartes's approach come to light. For Aristotle, the demonstrative syllogism was not an instrument of discovery but a heuristic device, and its epistemic value lay in its explanatory role, that is, epistemic and consequential directions were the contrary of each other. Although they were all regulated by topical reasoning, the means by which results were achieved varied from discipline to discipline, and experiment occasionally played a significant role, although this is true in the main of the biological sciences rather than physics and astronomy. Nevertheless, the difference between Aristotle and Descartes here is not as great as the latter would have us believe. Even more interesting, however, is the similarity between Aristotle's heuristic use of the demonstrative syllogism and Descartes's project of incorporating results achieved by problem-solving methods into the deductively organized system of natural philosophy of the *Principles*. Such a deductively organized system can, on Descartes's account, have no epistemic value in the sense of leading us from a knowledge of premisses to a knowledge of epistemically novel conclusions. But if, as in Aristotle's pedagogic use of demonstrative syllogisms, it is a question of their epistemic value lying in their ability to explain known results in terms of basic principles, then Descartes does appear to be allowing some kind of epistemic value to deduction. It is hard to see what the point of the *Principles* would be otherwise. What the explanation actually consists in differs in the two cases, of course: for Aristotle it takes the form of providing the relevant kinds of causes for complex phenomena, whereas in Descartes's case a very obscure and often contradictory account is offered because the complex relations between metaphysics and physics in his natural philosophy made it extremely difficult to identify causal factors.[8] Moreover, established truths in natural philosophy are extremely rare for Descartes (something he considers, of course, to be a temporary situation), whereas for Aristotle our knowledge in this area is virtually complete. Despite these differences, however, there is a striking similarity between the two approaches, and Descartes's differences from Aristotle at the methodological level are not as great as his apparently total rejection of Aristotle would lead us to believe.

Desmond Clarke has pointed out that it is 'highly unlikely that either Descartes or any of his followers accepted the almost farcical methodology with which they are traditionally credited'.[9] The irony is not only that the apriorist and deductivist methodology

---

[8] See e.g. M. Gueroult's exemplary account of the explanatory problems Descartes has with his notion of force in his 'The Metaphysics and Physics of Force in Descartes', in S. Gaukroger (ed.), *Descartes*, 196–229.

[9] D. Clarke, 'Pierre-Sylvain Régis: A Paradigm of Cartesian Methodology', *Archiv für Geschichte der Philosophie*, 62 (1980), 289.

ascribed to Descartes is vehemently rejected by him, but that his rejection goes too far. It effectively rules out deduction having any epistemic value. This in fact goes beyond what he can establish, and moreover it contradicts his own procedure in the *Principles*, whose deductive structure would be quite pointless unless deduction had some epistemic value. This is not simply a problem of 'method', as is usually thought, but something which has its roots at a much deeper level, in his notion of inference. If Descartes has an ambiguous position on method it is because he has failed to resolve the question of how arguments can be informative. This is, at least, what I have been concerned to show, and if I have been successful then we are forced to the conclusion that there is no real elucidation to be gained from asking what Descartes's conception of method was. His remarks on method cannot be reconciled because problems at a more fundamental level make it impossible to develop a coherent conception of method.

Conclusion

IN my discussion of Descartes's conception of inference I have
distinguished two different kinds of issue. The first, which I
looked at in Chapter 2, is a question about the nature of our grasp
of a deductive inference, and this is the concern of Descartes's
doctrine of *intuitus*. The second, which I looked at in Chapters 3
and 4, is a question about the epistemic value of deductive
inference in the contexts of mathematical and scientific enquiry,
and this is the concern of his doctrine of method. Given the
complexity of the questions raised by these doctrines, it may be
helpful to spell out in broader context what each of them involves
and what the relation between them is.

Descartes's doctrine of *intuitus* is directed towards a fundamental question about what inference consists in, and the approach that he adopts is best understood by contrasting it with
what I have called Aristotle's discursive conception of inference.
On this conception, logic is modelled upon rules for disputation,
where the point of making deductive inferences is to produce
compelling arguments, arguments which will be irresistible to
someone (or at least to someone who is rational) who accepts
certain premisses. In other words, the point of the exercise is to
induce conviction by argument, whether this conviction be
induced in an opponent, a student, or oneself. The conception is
discursive in that it is modelled on disputation, which necessarily
involves at least two people, and the exercise comes to an end when
conviction has been achieved. The rules underlying this logic
conceived on the model of disputation must obviously be uncontentious, but if challenged by a sceptic the appropriate form of
justification is similarly discursive: it consists in showing that they
must in fact be assumed if the sceptic is to be able to argue or even
state the sceptical case. Descartes's conception could not be

further from this. Inference is not conceived in terms of a discursive process but is explicitly something which cannot be analysed or explained. It is a paradigmatically mental operation by which one grasps connections between one's ideas. Understanding an inference consists, not in spelling out and analysing its steps, but in trying to bypass these steps altogether so that one can grasp the connection they exhibit in its own right, free from the mediation of logical steps, as it were. Moreover, there can be no question of justifying such an unmediated inference, for on Descartes's conception such a justification would be a justification to oneself—something designed to convince oneself and not, as on the discursive conception, an opponent—and this is not possible because our grasp of an inference in an *intuitus* is the most primitive and fundamental grasp we have.

Descartes's insistence on the primitive nature of inference (when grasped in an *intuitus*) is tied to his view that inferential connections (again when grasped in an *intuitus*) are self-evident. Something's being self-evident, for Descartes, means that it can neither be proved, explained, nor justified. This in turn means that he would have had to reject both Leibniz's proof of the self-evident truth that $2 + 2 = 4$ and Aristotle's justification of the self-evident principle of non-contradiction. His rejection of the former, I have argued, would have been along Lockean lines: that the premisses from which the purported proof derives are no more self-evident than the conclusion. But, as we have seen, this is irrelevant. Logic is concerned with the systematic relation between truths, it is concerned with capturing those inferential relations which are truth-preserving, not with establishing the less evident from the more evident, although particular deductions may have this epistemic property. The case of Aristotle's justification of the law of non-contradiction is rather different. Although it could not legitimately be claimed that the justification is more self-evident than what is being justified, or that the self-evidence of the law is increased as a result of the justification, the justification does, if accepted, mark an epistemic advance. It offers an account of the origin of the validity of, and perhaps even the self-evidence of, the law of non-contradiction. Yet it is clear that Descartes would not have accepted the proposed justification. What Aristotle's justification shows, at best, on the Cartesian account, is that we cannot get by without it, but this does not make it true. The only indicator of truth is clear and distinct perception, and we cannot ask *why* we have a clear and distinct perception of something any more than we can ask *why* we know truths. Clear and distinct perception is the means which an omnipotent God has given us by which to recognize (some) truths, where something is true if our idea of it corresponds to how it really is. More generally, a discursive argument works by getting someone to agree to something on the basis of shared premises. This is quite contrary to Descartes's approach for all it can achieve is conviction, not truth, and such conviction may be contrary to truth in many cases. As I have indicated, the discursive conception requires common ground between oneself and one's opponents, and in the context of early seventeenth-century natural philosophy this would not have been forthcoming. The polemical strength of Descartes's conception derives from the fact that the case against conceiving of inference in a discursive way is closely tied to the case against appealing in one's enquiries to what is generally accepted rather than to what is the case.

But of course such polemical strength is a function of local and temporary factors, and is not an indication of the intrinsic worth of Descartes's conception as an account of the nature of inference. How then does it compare with the discursive conception? The discursive model appears to have two outstanding problems in comparison to Descartes's conception. On the Cartesian account, inference cannot be justified, whereas Aristotle offers us a justification of the law of non-contradiction. But to justify one basic law inevitably opens up the question of whether and how the others are justified, and Aristotle offers no comprarable justification of the others: in fact, he makes no attempt at all at such justification. Indeed, it is difficult to imagine how, for example, there could be a convincing discursive justification of the law of the excluded middle along Aristotelian lines. Secondly, whatever our general model of inference, it has to be realized that inference is a cognitive operation, and any account which makes a claim to be complete must capture the cognitive aspects of inference. Aristotle's own account is very poor in this respect: his invoking of νοῦς in accounting for the difference between demonstrative and non-demonstrative syllogisms is wholly gratuitous, for example, and almost nothing is offered on cognitive questions of inference. On the other hand, as I have argued in detail, Descartes's account of the primitive nature of inference is highly problematic, and even where he offers convincing arguments (e.g. those in connection with Herbert of Cherbury's *De veritate*), the moral he draws from them is quite unwarranted, effectively ruling out the possibility of any understanding of inference. Moreover, when he raises cognitive issues about inference these tend to be in terms of a view that epistemic advance is the only criterion of the value of deduction, and deduction fails miserably by this criterion on his understanding of it. I have challenged this argument, and there can be little doubt that it marks a step back from Aristotle's position.

An overall comparative assessment would be easier if we ourselves had clear-cut answers to these kinds of questions, but in fact the issues are far from settled. One can find, indeed one cannot help but find, in the contemporary literature on inference, defences of accounts which are in many respects revised and more sophisticated versions of the discursive and facultative conceptions. Hintikka and others, in their game-theoretic semantics, have developed an approach to inference which, while influenced by Wittgenstein rather than Aristotle, is strikingly similar to the discursive conception.[1] Ellis, on the other hand, has recently revived the view central to the facultative model that 'the laws of logic are the laws of thought', and defended a conception which is in some ways a sophisticated development of the tradition of thinking about inference from Descartes to Mill.[2] And in an account such as Dummett's, which steers more of a middle course in trying to capture both the logical and cognitive aspects of

---

[1] Cf. e.g. the contributions to E. Saarinen (ed.), *Game-Theoretical Semantics* (Dordrecht, 1978).
[2] Cf. B. Ellis, *Rational Belief Systems* (Oxford, 1979).

inference, one can sense the pull of constraints imposed by discursive and facultative conceptions.[3]

The polemical strength of Descartes's conception lies, I have said, in its association with 'method', with the experimental and problem-solving approach that he advocates. I have challenged the apriorist and deductivist interpretation of Descartes's method, and it is worth remembering that Descartes was considered in the later seventeenth century as the great defender of the hypothetical method.[4] This has not been the prevalent view in the twentieth century, however, where he has been thought to have adopted an approach whereby all scientific knowledge is somehow to be deduced from the *cogito*.[5] In so far as this interpretation depends upon a preoccupation with his doctrine of ideas, however, some of the blame can be traced back to the seventeenth century, and particularly to Arnauld and Nicole's *Port-Royal Logic* (1662), where a geometrical model of invention is proposed which depends very much on reflecting upon what is contained in one's own ideas.[6] This model plays down observation and experiment, although, rather interestingly, Arnauld advocates probabilistic reasoning (Chapter 23 of Part IV)[7] on grounds almost identical to those of the sixteenth-century humanist apologists for history that I looked at in Chapter 1. Whatever its affinities with Descartes's own programme, the *Port-Royal Logic* departs from his conception of method in crucial respects, and not all of these constitute improvements.

The discrepancy between Descartes's conception of method, on the prevalent view that this consists in the deduction of scientific truths from the *cogito*, and his explicit rejection of syllogistic and synthetic forms of demonstration is obvious, but a commitment to

[3] Cf. M. Dummett, 'The Justification of Deduction', in his *Truth and Other Enigmas* (London, 1978), 290–318.
[4] Cf. the discussion in ch. 5 of L. Lauden, *Science and Hypothesis* (Dordrecht, 1981).
[5] This view can be traced back at least to K. Fischer, *History of Modern Philosophy: Descartes and his School* (London, 1887).
[6] This approach is even more marked in Arnauld's *Des vraies et des fausses idées*, e.g. ch. 6.
[7] Cf. the discussion in ch. 9 of I. Hacking, *The Emergence of Probability* (Cambridge, 1975). Hacking doubts whether Arnauld is in fact the author of the chapters on probability.

the former view has not encouraged serious discussion of the latter, as might have been expected. The import and role of the latter doctrine has therefore remained somewhat mysterious, and in trying to clear up this mystery I hope I have also clarified what he himself saw as one of his great philosophical achievements, his doctrine of method.

Bibliography

This bibliography lists books and articles referred to in the text, as well as a few items that I have found especially helpful but have not specifically referred to. Reasonably full bibliographies can be found in the items marked with an asterisk.

AGRICOLA, RUDOLPH, *De inventione dialectica libri tres, cum scholiis Joannis Matthaei Phrissemii* (Paris, 1529).

AQUINAS, THOMAS, *On the Unity of the Intellect Against the Averroists*, ed. and trans. Beatrice H. Zedler (Milwaukee, 1968).

ARISTOTLE, *Aristotle's Metaphysics*, ed. W. D. Ross (2 vols., Oxford, 1924).

—— *Aristotle's Physics*, ed. W. D. Ross (Oxford, 1936).

—— *Aristotle's Prior and Posterior Analytics*, ed. W. D. Ross (Oxford, 1949).

—— *Categoriae et Liber de interpretatione*, ed. L. Minio Paluello (Oxford, 1974).

—— *Topica et Sophistici elenchi*, ed. W. D. Ross (Oxford, 1974).

ARNAULD, ANTOINE, *Logique de Port Royal, Objections contre les Méditations de Descartes, Traité des vraies et des fausses idées, par Arnauld*, ed. C. Jourdain (Paris, 1846).

ASHWORTH, EARLINE J., *Language and Logic in the Post-Medieval Period* (Dordrecht, 1974), 787–96.

—— 'The Eclipse of Medieval Logic', in Norman Kretzman, Anthony Kenny, and Jan Pinborg (eds.), *The Cambridge History of Later Medieval Philosophy* (Cambridge, 1982).

AVERSA, RAPHAEL, *Logica* (Rome, 1623).

BACON, FRANCIS, *The Works of Francis Bacon*, ed. J. Spedding, R. L. Ellis, and D. D. Heath (7 vols., London, 1887–92).

BALME, DAVID M., *Aristotle's De partibus animalium I and De generatione animalium I* (Oxford, 1972).

BARNES, JONATHAN, 'Aristotle's Theory of Demonstration', in Jonathan Barnes, Malcolm Schofield, and Richard Sorabji (eds.), *Articles on Aristotle*, i: *Science* (London, 1975), 65–87.

BARNES, J., 'Proof Destroyed', in Malcolm Schofield, Myles Burnyeat, and Jonathan Barnes (eds.), *Doubt and Dogmatism: Studies in Hellenistic Epistemology* (Oxford, 1980), 161–81.

BECK, LESLIE JOHN, *The Method of Descartes: A Study of the Regulae* (Oxford, 1952).

BELAVAL, YVON, *Leibniz: Critique de Descartes* (Paris, 1960).

BLAKE, RALPH M., DUCASSE, CURT J., and MADDEN, EDWARD J., *Theories of Scientific Method* (Seattle, 1960).

BLANCH, JOSEPHUS, *Commentarii in universam Aristotelis logicam* (Valentia, 1612).

BOOLE, GEORGE, *The Mathematical Analysis of Logic* (Cambridge, 1847).

BROWN, STUART, *Leibniz* (Sussex, 1984).

BRUNSCHWIG, JACQUES, 'Proof Defined', in Malcolm Schofield, Myles Burnyeat, and Jonathan Barnes (eds.), *Doubt and Dogmatism: Studies in Hellenistic Epistemology* (Oxford, 1980), 125–60.

BUCHDAHL, GERD, 'Descartes' Anticipation of a "Logic of Scientific Discovery"', in A. C. Crombie (ed.), *Scientific Change* (London, 1963), 399–417.

—— 'The Relevance of Descartes' Philosophy for Modern Philosophy of Science', *British Journal for the History of Science*, 1 (1963), 227–49.

—— *Metaphysics and the Philosophy of Science* (Oxford, 1969).

BUICKEROOD, JAMES G., 'The Natural History of the Understanding: Locke and the Rise of Facultative Logic in the Eighteenth Century', *History and Philosophy of Logic*, 6 (1985), 157–90.

CABERO, CHRYSOSTOMUS, *Brevis summularum recapitulatio* (Valladolid, 1623).

CAMPBELL, GEORGE, *The Philosophy of Rhetoric: In Two Volumes* (London and Edinburgh, 1776).

CASILIUS, ANTONIUS, *Introductio in Aristotelis logicam* (Tomae, 1629).

CASSIRER, ERNST, KRISTELLER, PAUL OSKAR, RANDALL, JOHN HERMAN, jun. (eds.), *The Renaissance Philosophy of Man* (Chicago, 1948).

CATON, HIRAM, *The Origin of Subjectivity* (New Haven, 1973).

CHAPPELL, VERE, and DONEY, WILLIS, *Twenty-five Years of Descartes Scholarship, 1960–1984* (New York, 1987).

CHARLTON, WILLIAM, *Aristotle's Physics, I, II* (Oxford, 1970).

CICERO, Loeb edn. of the *Writings* (28 vols., Cambridge, Mass., 1933–).

CLARKE, DESMOND M., 'Pierre-Sylvain Régis: A Paradigm of Cartesian Methodology', *Archiv für Geschichte der Philosophie*, 62 (1980), 289–310.

—— *Descartes' Philosophy of Science* (Manchester, 1982).

COLISH, MARCIA L., *The Stoic Tradition from Antiquity to the Early Middle Ages* (2 vols., Leiden, 1985).

COMPOTISTA, GARLANDUS, *Dialectica*, ed. L. M. de Rijk (Assen, 1959).

CORCORAN, JOHN, 'Remarks on Stoic Deduction', in John Corcoran (ed.), *Ancient Logic and its Modern Interpretations* (Dordrecht, 1974), 169–81.

COUTURAT, LOUIS, *La Logique de Leibniz d'après des documents inédits* (Paris, 1901).

CURTIUS, ERNST ROBERT, *European Literature and the Latin Middle Ages* (Princeton, 1973).

DENISSOFF, ÉLIE, *Descartes, premier théorician de la physique mathématique* (Louvain and Paris, 1970).

DESCARTES, RENÉ, *Œuvres de Descartes*, ed. Charles Adam and Paul Tannery (11 vols., Paris, 1974–86).

—— *Œuvres philosophiques*, ed. Ferdinand Alquié (3 vols., Paris, 1963–73).

DUMMETT, MICHAEL, 'The Justification of Deduction', in Michael Dummett, *Truth and Other Enigmas* (London, 1978), 290–318.

ELLIS, BRIAN, *Rational Belief Systems* (Oxford, 1979).

FISCHER, KUNO, *History of Modern Philosophy: Descartes and his School* (London, 1887).

FONSECA, PETRUS, *Institutionem dialecticarum libri octo* (Lisbon, 1564).

FRANKFURT, HARRY G., *Demons, Dreamers, and Madmen* (Indianapolis, 1970).

—— 'Descartes on the Consistency of Reason', in Michael Hooker (ed.), *Descartes: Critical and Interpretive Essays* (Baltimore, 1978), 26–39.

FRANKLIN, JULIAN H., *Jean Bodin and the Sixteenth Century Revolution in the Methodology of Law and History* (New York, 1963).

FREGE, GOTTLOB, *The Foundations of Arithmetic* (Oxford, 1959).

FUMAROLI, MARC, *L'Âge de l'éloquence: Rhétorique et 'res literati' de la renaissance au seuil de l'époque classique* (Geneva, 1980).

GASSENDI, PIERRE, *Pierre Gassendi's Institutio logica (1658)*, ed. and trans. Howard Jones (Assen, 1981).

GAUKROGER, STEPHEN, 'Aristotle on Intelligible Matter', *Phronesis*, 25 (1980), 187–97.

—— 'Descartes' Project for a Mathematical Physics', in Stephen Gaukroger (ed.), *Descartes: Philosophy, Mathematics and Physics* (Sussex, 1980), 97–140.

GAUKROGER, S., 'The One and the Many: Aristotle on the Individuation of Numbers', *Classical Quarterly*, NS 22 (1982), 312–22.

—— 'Vico and the Maker's Knowledge Principle', *History of Philosophy Quarterly*, 3 (1986), 29–44.

—— 'Descartes' Conception of Inference', in Roger Woolhouse (ed.), *Metaphysics and the Philosophy of Science in the Seventeenth and Eighteenth Centuries* (Dordrecht, 1988), 101–32.

GEWIRTH, ALAN, 'Clearness and Distinctness in Descartes', *Philosophy*, 18 (1943), 17–36.

—— 'The Cartesian Circle Reconsidered', *Journal of Philosophy*, 67 (1970), 668–85.

GIBSON, JAMES, *Locke's Theory of Knowledge and its Historical Relations* (Cambridge, 1931).

GILBERT, NEAL W., *Renaissance Concepts of Method* (New York, 1960).

GILSON, ÉTIENNE, *La Liberté chez Descartes et la théologie* (Paris, 1913).

—— *Études sur le rôle de la pensée médiévale dans la formation du système cartésien* (Paris, 1930).

—— *Descartes: Discours de la méthode, texte et commentaire* (Paris, 1962).

GOULD, JOSIAH, 'Deduction in Stoic Logic', in John Corcoran (ed.), *Ancient Logic and its Modern Interpretations* (Dordrecht, 1974), 151–68.

GROSHOLZ, EMILY, 'Descartes' Unification of Algebra and Geometry', in Stephen Gaukroger (ed.), *Descartes: Philosophy, Mathematics and Physics* (Sussex, 1980), 156–68.

GUEROULT, MARTIAL, 'The Metaphysics and Physics of Force in Descartes', in Stephen Gaukroger (ed.), *Descartes: Philosophy, Mathematics and Physics* (Sussex, 1980), 196–229.

HACKING, IAN, *The Emergence of Probability* (Cambridge, 1975).

—— 'What is Logic?', *Journal of Philosophy*, 76 (1979), 285–319.

—— 'Proof and Eternal Truths: Descartes and Leibniz', in Stephen Gaukroger (ed.), *Descartes: Philosophy, Mathematics and Physics* (Sussex, 1980), 169–80.

—— 'A Leibnizian Theory of Truth', in Michael Hooker (ed.), *Leibniz: Critical and Interpretive Essays* (Manchester, 1982), 185–95.

HARVEY, E. RUTH, *The Inward Wits: Psychological Theory in the Middle Ages and the Renaissance* (London, 1975).

HINTIKKA, JAAKO, 'A Discourse on Descartes' Method', in Michael Hooker (ed.), *Descartes: Critical and Interpretive Essays* (Baltimore, 1978).

—— and REMES, UNTO, *The Method of Analysis* (Dordrecht, 1974).

HOBBES, THOMAS, *The English Works of Thomas Hobbes*, ed. Sir William Molesworth (11 vols., London, 1839–45).

HOWELL, WILBUR SAMUEL, *Logic and Rhetoric in England, 1500–1700* (Princeton, 1956).

—— *Eighteenth-Century British Logic and Rhetoric* (Princeton, 1971).

JAEGER, WERNER, *Paideia: The Ideals of Greek Culture* (3 vols., Oxford, 1939–45).

JARDINE, LISA, 'Humanism and the Teaching of Logic', in Norman Kretzman, Anthony Kenny, and Jan Pinborg (eds.), *The Cambridge History of Later Medieval Philosophy* (Cambridge, 1982), 797–807.

—— 'Lorenzo Valla: Academic Skepticism and the New Humanist Dialectic', in Myles Burnyeat (ed.), *The Skeptical Tradition* (Berkeley, 1983), 253–86.

JARDINE, NICHOLAS, 'Galileo's Road of Truth and the Demonstrative Regress', *Studies in History and Philosophy of Science*, 7 (1976), 277–318.

KAMES, HENRY HOME, Lord KAMES, *Introduction to the Art of Thinking* (Edinburgh, 1761).

KAPP, ERNEST, 'Syllogistic', in Jonathan Barnes, Malcolm Schofield, and Richard Sorabji (eds.), *Articles on Aristotle*, i: *Science* (London, 1975), 35–49.

KLEIN, JACOB, *Greek Mathematical Thought and the Origin of Algebra* (Cambridge, Mass., 1968).

KNEALE, WILLIAM, 'The Province of Logic', in H. D. Lewis (ed.), *Contemporary British Philosophy, Third Series* (London, 1956), 235–62.

—— and MARTHA, *The Development of Logic* (Oxford, 1962).

KRETZMAN, NORMAN, 'Semantics, History of', in P. Edwards (ed.), *The Encyclopedia of Philosophy* (8 vols., New York, 1967), vii. 358–406.

LACHTERMAN, DAVID R., '*Objectum Purae Matheseos*: Mathematical Construction and the Passage from Essence to Existence', in Amelie Oksenberg Rorty (ed.), *Essays on Descartes' Meditations* (Berkeley, 1986), 435–58.

LARMORE, CHARLES, 'Descartes' Empirical Epistemology', in Stephen Gaukroger (ed.), *Descartes: Philosophy, Mathematics and Physics* (Sussex, 1980), 6–22.

—— 'Descartes' Psychologistic Theory of Assent', *History of Philosophy Quarterly*, 1 (1984), 61–74.

LAUDAN, LARRY, *Science and Hypothesis* (Dordrecht, 1981).

LEAR, JONATHAN, *Aristotle and Logical Theory* (Cambridge, 1980).

LEIBNIZ, GOTTFRIED WILHELM, *Die mathematische Schriften von G. W. Leibniz*, ed. C. I. Gerhardt (7 vols., Berlin and Halle, 1849–63).

——*Die philosophischen Schriften von G. W. Leibniz*, ed. C. I. Gerhardt (7 vols., Berlin, 1875–90).

——*Opuscules et fragments inédits de Leibniz*, ed. Louis Couturat (Paris, 1903).

LENOBLE, ROBERT, *Mersenne ou la naissance de mécanisme* (2nd edn., Paris, 1971).

LOCKE, JOHN, *An Essay Concerning Human Understanding*, ed. Alexander Campbell Fraser (2 vols., Oxford, 1957).

ŁUKASIEWCZ, JAN, *Aristotle's Syllogistic from the Standpoint of Modern Formal Logic* (Oxford, 1957).

MAHONEY, MICHAEL, *The Mathematical Career of Pierre de Fermat* (Princeton, 1973).

MARION, JEAN-LUC, *Sur l'ontologie grise de Descartes* (Paris, 1981).

——*Sur la théologie blanche de Descartes* (Paris, 1981).

MATES, BENSON, *Stoic Logic* (Berkeley, 1961).

MAULA, ERKKA, 'An End of Invention', *Annals of Science*, 38 (1981), 109–22.

MAULL, NANCY L., 'Cartesian Optics and the Geometrization of Nature', in Stephen Gaukroger (ed.), *Descartes: Philosophy, Mathematics and Physics* (Sussex, 1980), 23–40.

MILL, JOHN STUART, *A System of Logic* (8th edn., London, 1967).

MITTLESTRASS, JÜRGEN, 'The Philosopher's Conception of "Mathesis Universalis" from Descartes to Leibniz', *Annals of Science*, 36 (1979), 593–610.

MUELLER, IAN, 'Greek Mathematics and Greek Logic', in John Corcoran (ed.), *Ancient Logic and its Modern Interpretations* (Dordrecht, 1974), 35–70.

——'Geometry and Scepticism' in Jonathan Barnes, Jacques Brunschwig, Myles Burnyeat, and Malcolm Schofield (eds.), *Science and Speculation: Studies in Hellenistic Theory and Practice* (Cambridge, 1982), 69–95.

NUCHELMANS, GABRIEL, *Late Scholastic and Humanist Theories of the Proposition* (Amsterdam, 1980).

ONG, WALTER J., 'Hobbes and Talon's Ramist Rhetoric in English', *Transactions of the Cambridge Bibliographical Society*, 1 (1951), 260–9.

—— *Ramus, Method, and the Decay of Dialogue* (Cambridge, Mass., 1958).

—— **Ramus and Talon Inventory* (Cambridge, Mass., 1958).

OWEN, GWILYM ELLIS LANE, 'Tithenai ta phainomena', in Jonathan Barnes, Malcolm Schofield, and Richard Sorabji (eds.), *Articles on Aristotle*, I: *Science* (London, 1975), 113–26.

PAGEL, WALTER, 'Medieval and Renaissance Contributions to the Knowledge of the Brain and its Functions', in F. N. L. Poynter (ed.), *The History and Philosophy of Knowledge of the Brain and its Functions* (Oxford, 1958), 95–114.

PASSMORE, JOHN A., 'Descartes, the British Empiricists and Formal Logic', *Philosophical Review*, 62 (1953), 543–53.

PATZIG, GÜNTHER, *Die aristotelische Syllogistik* (2nd edn., Göttingen, 1963).

PEGHAIRE, J., *Intellectus et ratio selon S. Thomas d'Aquin* (Paris and Ottawa, 1936).

PETER OF SPAIN, *Tractatus called afterwards Summule logicales*, ed. L. M. de Rijk (Assen, 1972).

PIGEAUD, JACKIE, *La Maladie de l'âme: Étude sur la relation de l'âme et du corps dans la tradition médico-philosophique antique* (Paris, 1981).

POMPANAZZI, PIETRO, *De immortalitate animae* (Bologna, 1516).

POPKIN, RICHARD H., *The History of Scepticism from Erasmus to Spinoza* (Berkeley, 1979).

PRANTL, KARL, *Geschichte der Logik im Abendlande* (4 vols., Leipzig, 1855–70).

PYCIOR, HELENA M., 'Mathematics and Philosophy: Wallis, Hobbes, Barrow, and Berkeley', *Journal of the History of Ideas*, 48 (1987), 265–86.

RAMUS, PETER, *Aristotelicae animadversiones* (Paris, 1543).

—— *Dialecticae institutiones* (Paris, 1546).

—— *Scholae in liberales artes* (Paris, 1569).

RANDALL, JOHN HERMAN, jun., *The School of Padua and the Emergence of Modern Science* (Padua, 1961).

REIF, PATRICIA, 'The Textbook Tradition in Natural Philosophy, 1600–1650', *Journal of the History of Ideas*, 30 (1969), 17–32.

RISSE, WILHELM, 'Zur Vorgeschichte der cartesischen Methodenlehre', *Archiv für Geschichte der Philosophie*, 45 (1963), 269–91.

—— *Die Logik der Neuzeit*, i: *1500–1640* (Stuttgart and Bad Cannstatt, 1964).

RISSE, W., *Bibliographia logica: Verzeichnis der Druckschriften zur Logik mit Angabe ihre Fundorte, i: 1472–1800 (Hildesheim, 1965).

ROSSI, PAOLO, Clavis universalis: Arti mnemoniche e logica combinatoria da Lullo a Leibniz (Milan and Naples, 1960).

ROTH, LEON, Descartes' Discourse on Method (Oxford, 1937).

SAARINEN, ESA (ed.), Game-Theoretical Semantics (Dordrecht, 1978).

SCHMITT, CHARLES B., Cicero scepticus (The Hague, 1972).

—— 'The Rediscovery of Ancient Scepticism in Modern Times', in Myles Burnyeat (ed.), The Skeptical Tradition (Berkeley, 1983).

SCHÜLING, HERMANN, *Bibliographie der psychologischen Literatur des 16. Jh. (Hildesheim, 1967).

SCHUSTER, JOHN A., 'Descartes and the Scientific Revolution, 1618–1634', Ph.D. thesis (Princeton University, 1977).

—— 'Descartes' Mathesis Universalis, 1619–28', in Stephen Gaukroger (ed.), Descartes: Philosophy, Mathematics and Physics (Sussex, 1980), 41–96.

SCOTT, J. F., The Scientific Work of René Descartes (London, 1976).

SEBBA, GREGOR, *Bibliographia cartesiana: A Critical Guide to the Descartes Literature, 1800–1960 (The Hague, 1964).

SEXTUS EMPIRICUS, Loeb edn. of the Writings (4 vols., Cambridge, Mass., 1933–9).

SKULSKY, HAROLD, 'Paduan Epistemology and the Doctrine of One Mind', Journal for the History of Philosophy, 6 (1968), 341–61.

STEWART, DUGALD, The Collected Works of Dugald Stewart, ed. Sir William Hamilton (11 vols., Edinburgh, 1854–60).

STUMP, ELEONORE, Boethius' De topicis differentiis (Ithaca, 1978).

—— 'Garlandus Compotista and Dialectic in the Eleventh and Twelfth Centuries', History and Philosophy of Logic, 1 (1980), 1–18.

STYAZHKIN, N. I., History of Mathematical Logic from Leibniz to Peano (Cambridge, Mass., 1969).

SUAREZ, FRANCISCUS, Metaphysicarum disputatione, tomi duo (Salamanca, 1597).

SZABÓ, ARPÁD, 'Working Backwards and Proving by Synthesis', Appendix I to Jaako Hintikka and Unto Remes, The Method of Analysis (Dordrecht, 1974), 118–30.

—— 'Analysis und Synthesis', Acta classica universitas scientiarum bebreceniensis, 10/11 (1974–5), 155–64.

TOLETUS, FRANCISCUS, Introductio in dialecticam Aristotelis (Rome, 1560).

TRINKAUS, CHARLES, *In Our Image and Likeness: Humanity and Divinity in Italian Humanist Thought* (2 vols., London, 1970).

VASOLI, CESARE, *La dialettica e la retorica dell'umanesimo: Invenzione e metodo nella cultura del XV–XVI secolo* (Milan, 1968).

VERBEKE, GERARD, *L'Évolution de la doctrine du pneuma du Stoïcisme à S. Augustin* (Paris and Louvain, 1945).

VUILLEMIN, JACQUES, *Mathématiques et metaphysique chez Descartes* (Paris, 1960).

WEBER, JEAN-PAUL, *La Constitution du texte des Regulae* (Paris, 1964).

WEIL, E., 'The Place of Logic in Aristotle's Thought', in Jonathan Barnes, Malcolm Schofield, and Richard Sorabji (eds.), *Articles on Aristotle*, i: *Science* (London, 1975), 88–112.

WILKINS, JOHN, *Essay Towards a Real Character and a Philosophical Language* (London, 1668).

WILLIAMS, BERNARD, *Descartes: The Project of Pure Enquiry* (Harmondsworth, 1978).

YATES, FRANCES, A., *The Art of Memory* (Harmondsworth, 1978).

YOLTON, JOHN W., *Perceptual Acquaintance from Descartes to Reid* (Oxford, 1984).

Index